COMMIE COWBOYS

The Bourgeoisie and the Nation-State in the Western Genre

Revised, Second Edition

Ryan W. McMaken

Foreword by Paul A. Cantor

For Jessica.

CONTENTS

FOREWORD

The Western, having long been pronounced dead, has recently shown signs of coming back to life in American popular culture. The HBO television series *Deadwood* (2004-2006) demonstrated without question that creative possibilities remain in a genre that had seemed to be exhausted. The critical and commercial success of the Coen Brothers' remake of the movie *True Grit* (2010) offered more testimony to the vitality of the Western. Most recently, the History Channel's *Hatfields & McCoys* (2012) drew viewers in such numbers that TV executives throughout the industry took notice. Although the Western has not returned to the extraordinary level of popularity it enjoyed in the middle of the twentieth century, a trickle of films and TV shows in the genre seems to have turned into a steady stream. We may well be entering a new age of the Western.

And that should not surprise us. The Western has always been the most distinctively American of pop culture genres, and has served Americans well in their attempts to come to grips with their experience as a nation. To be sure, many Western films and TV shows are exactly what people have in mind when they speak of mindless entertainment, but it is remarkable how often the genre has facilitated the serious exploration of some of America's central social and political problems. In the sharp dramatic confrontations that the Western invites and in fact demands, a film or a TV show can raise such issues as the individual vs. the community, freedom vs. order, or the vigilante vs. the law. Studying the Western can tell us a great deal about how Americans understand themselves and the political community in which they live. At a moment when the issue of freedom is being debated anew in American political discourse, it is understandable that the Western is coming back to life.

Ryan McMaken's *Commie Cowboys* helps us to sort out what the Western has meant over the years in American popular culture and to understand why the genre might be currently undergoing a revival. He provides a thoughtful and wide-ranging analysis of the Western, principally in films, but with some examples of TV series and even a few references to fiction. The book goes all the way back to Western films in the silent era and comes forward almost to the present day. The heart of the book is an analysis of the classic Westerns of John Ford, Howard Hawks, and Anthony Mann and of the revisionist work of such directors as Sergio Leone, Sam Peckinpah, and Clint Eastwood. One does not have to agree with every one of McMaken's interpretations of individual films to profit from his attempt to make sense of the genre as a whole.

Academic critics of the Western have tended to view it as a politically conservative genre and to argue that it offers a prime example of the American capitalist entertainment industry self-servingly providing ideological support for capitalism. The rugged individualist as hero in the Western is often viewed in Cultural Studies as an icon of the solo competitor in a market economy. McMaken's book is particularly valuable for challenging this one-sided interpretation of the Western as a genre. The fact that the two most famous stars of Westerns, John Wayne and Clint Eastwood, have been identified with politically conservative causes may have misled critics into thinking that the genre itself is inherently conservative. In fact, the American West has proved fertile ground for liberal and even left-wing storytelling. As McMaken shows, Westerns have often developed anti-capitalist ideological positions. Crooked and corrupt businessmen people the frontier in many Westerns. In particular, owning land, especially large tracts of land, is often presented as the epitome of evil in Westerns, which tend to take the side of the little guy—the dirt farmer, the sheepherder, or the shopkeeper. Often some kind of public official—a sheriff, a U.S. marshal, or a frontier military commander—is shown to be necessary to curb the greed and selfishness of a cattle baron or a saloon owner. At the same time, many Westerns celebrate the power of government, specifically the federal government. When they ask how the West was won, often their answer is: through federal land grants and the building of the transcontinental railroad on the basis of federal subsidies. It is no accident that the man who made many of the classic Western films—John Ford—also made the classic New Deal tearjerker, *The Grapes of Wrath*. And would Kevin Costner ever have gotten involved in a genre that is politically conservative by nature?

With his perceptive analyses and steady accumulation of evidence, McMaken makes us take a fresh look at the Western and re-evaluate its place in American popular culture. Whatever your ultimate take on the Western may be, you will never look at it quite the same way after reading this book.

Paul A. Cantor
Harvard University, Cambridge
October 2012

PREFACE

My first job was on a cattle ranch near Elbert, Colorado when I was fourteen years old. I dug postholes and tightened fences and cleaned tack and shoveled manure. They gave me an old powder-blue Ford pickup truck to drive around. The transmission didn't work terribly well, so I had to make sure I never put the truck in a place where I would need to use reverse.

While I never thought that I'd be getting into any gunfights with outlaws, or doing anything incredibly exciting when I took that job, I was nevertheless struck by how tedious the work truly was. Few things ever happened that one would want to actually record in any Western film that featured cattle ranches or cattle barons. Even if I had worked on that ranch a hundred years earlier, and had been subject to all the hazards of the frontier, the work would have been largely the same, and not likely to be punctuated by any range wars or Indian wars.

The real story of the West was one of tedium and repetitive agricultural and mining work, of course, and not of showdowns on Main Street. Most people know on some level that Westerns are really very fanciful when compared to the real-life West, but I've come to realize that Westerns aren't really about the West at all. They're just myths that use a frontier setting to make a point through literature. That point is often political.

This book comes out of a combined interest in Western films and the intellectual history of nineteenth-century America. I began to wonder what the political ideologies were of the people who actually rode in covered wagons across the plains, and it gradually became clear that there was a big difference between the world view contained in a Western from the mid-twentieth century, and the world view of the people who actually settled the Western part of North America during the nineteenth century.

L.P. Hartley wrote that "the past is a foreign country, they do things differently there," and this is certainly true of America's past. The Westerns of the twentieth century we've come to think of as the defining, classical form of the genre are really about the twentieth century, and the nineteenth century can be barely glimpsed in the background of a Western from 1955 or 1960.

This isn't a novel observation of course, but I like to think that some of the observations in this book will contribute something new to how we look at Westerns.

Having been active in the libertarian movement for more than fifteen years, I've long been told that Westerns are inherently pro-capitalist and freedom-loving films. Yet, when I started to really watch them, I found that to not be the case at all. Westerns, just as often as not, tend to be anti-capitalist and authoritarian, which might explain why some *conservatives* like them, but it's hard to understand why any libertarian would ever want to identify Westerns as a whole with his own ideology.

That's not to say that Westerns aren't incredibly entertaining to watch. The final showdown in *The Good, The Bad, and the Ugly* is among the most entertaining eight minutes ever put on film, and as a kid, I must have watched *Silverado* more than twenty times. I also know about every word of Louis L'amour's exciting short novel *The Tall Stranger*, which, by the way, was made into a very boring movie in 1957.

But fundamentally, the Western is a genre that favors coercion over reason and war over peace. My readers can decide if that's a good thing or not.

This book began as an essay published at the libertarian web site *LewRockwell.com* about eight years ago. That essay turned out to be guilty of over-generalizing, and was in many ways incomplete. This book is a greatly expanded, updated, revised, and improved version of that essay. Since 2005, newly published criticism of the Western genre has justified a new look at the old essay. I have expanded several sections and added a new section on the *Little House on the Prairie* series and Rose Wilder Lane, plus dozens of explanatory and bibliographical notes.

Ryan McMaken
Denver, Colorado
November 2012

ACKNOWLEDGMENTS

Although I didn't realize it at the time, I received a pretty decent education at the University of Colorado, in spite of my best efforts to learn nothing. Faculty members Fred Glahe and Thad Tecza were particularly effective in ensuring that I now continue to read books even when I don't have to.

This book would almost certainly not exist without Lew Rockwell who has offered much encouragement and done much to make me a better writer over the past decade.

Thanks to the Social Science Department at Arapahoe Community College for providing me with a place to teach over the past eight years. The fear of looking like a fool in front of my students has done much to improve my understanding of many things.

Thanks to Alison O'Kelly who read and edited the manuscript, and better yet, did it for cheap.

I'm also thankful for my friends Derek Johnson and Myles Kantor whose correspondence and conversation have done much to improve my understanding of popular culture, among other things.

But most of all, I owe thanks to my wife Jessica, without whom I wouldn't have accomplished much of anything over the past thirteen years.

Introduction

In 1916, Charles Goodnight, an aging rancher who had lived the history of the great cattle drives across the plains, made a movie about the West. His film, *Old Texas*, featured no showdowns, no saloons, and no bandits. It was a tale of the West as remembered by a man who lived it. *Old Texas*, which is now lost, never found an audience. By 1916, the Western film had already been taking shape for more than a decade, and the gunmen, the hostile Indians, and the final showdown were rapidly becoming the dominant images of the American frontier in film. The primitive landscape, the moral certainty, and the violence of the Western dominated cinemas for decades more.

As a real-life frontiersman, what Goodnight didn't realize was that few Americans of the twentieth century were interested in the story of the real West. They were interested in a version of the West that consisted of fables featuring the gunfighter in a wild land. Eventually, the story of the gunfighter would dominate popular culture during the twentieth century and be unequaled in popularity by any other genre of film. The Western became the American popular art form at mid-century.

Although Westerns no longer dominate the airwaves, the gunfighter, whether in the form of a cavalryman, sheriff, or wandering frontiersman, retains his position as a powerful political and cultural symbol. Many fans of the Western have long contended that there is something inherently American at the core of the Western genre, and that the taming of a wild land and the civilizing force of the gunman embodies what the United States is and what it proposes to do across the globe.

To this day, politicians, artists, and military officers employ imagery of the American cowboy and gunfighter for political effect. Many treatments of the Western have explored the close connection between the Western genre and American politics and culture in great detail. Tom

Engelhardt, for example, writes extensively in *The End of Victory Culture* on the importance of the Western to American narratives glorifying World War II and justifying the Cold War.[1]

According to Engelhardt, during the immediate post-war period especially, the Western repeatedly invoked the image of the gunfighter as an affirmation of the proper role of the American state in the establishment of an American value system both in the old American West and worldwide.

With the onset of the Second World War, and into the 1950s and 60s, millions of Americans learned through their popular culture that peace and order are not obtainable without the efforts of the gunfighter and his ability to pave the way for civilization.

Although the gunfighter is most associated with the version made popular during the 1950s and 60s, the nuances of the gunfighter's place in society have varied over time from Owen Wister's 1902 novel *The Virginian* to Clint Eastwood's 1992 film *Unforgiven*.[2] Even before *The Virginian* began to make its influence felt in both literary circles and in the mass market for popular middlebrow fiction, the old frontier-themed dime novels were already being translated to the big screen in some of the earliest silent films made.[3] All of

---

[1] Thomas Engelhardt, *The End of Victory Culture: Cold War America and the Disillusioning of a Generation* (New York, NY: HarperCollins, 1995).

[2] *The Virginian* is widely regarded as the first true Western novel. While dime novels had included Western themes for many years, it was *The Virginian* by Wister and Grey's *Riders of the Purple Sage* that set the stage for the Western as serious adult literature beyond the comic-book-like world of the dime novels. The book would prove to be immensely influential on later Western film and fiction.

[3] One of the first silent films ever made was a Western: *The Great Train Robbery* in 1903. *The Virginian*, the novel credited with doing so much to create the genre, had been published only one year earlier in 1902.

the elements we now associate with classical Westerns took time to develop, however. Early silent Westerns of the 1900s, 10s and 20s, and then the Western B-movies of the 1930s, borrowed much from earlier dime novels, from the frontier works of James Fenimore Cooper, and even from nineteenth-century Victorian literature. As the twentieth century progressed, the genre slowly developed into what we consider to be the "traditional" or "classical" Westerns that are well-known today. By World War II, the genre had developed into the form that would come to dominate television and film so completely that by 1959, "adult" Western programming would make up almost one-quarter of all network nightly offerings.[4]

Since the Vietnam War, the status of the Western as the dominant genre of American popular culture has declined, and the gunfighter of the classical Westerns is now often viewed by many Americans as a symbol of a sexist and racist American value system that is best left in the past.[5] At the same time, many Americans who look with favor on what they perceive to be traditional American values are likely to regard the Western with a nostalgic eye and as a genre that preserves the values of earlier and presumably more virtuous generations.

In the modern political culture wars, this has led to a case in which the American right wing is likely to look to Westerns as a laudable genre, while the left regards is as a relic of a more unjust age. Film critic Robert Ray, writing on "left and right" cycles in Hollywood moviemaking, regards post-war Westerns as part of the "right" cycle in films, and points to later films such as *Dirty Harry*, which capitalize on

---

[4] Engelhardt, p. 89

[5] For a more even-handed discussion of this topic, see John G.Cawelti, *The Six-Gun Mystique Sequel*, (Bowling Green, OH: Bowling Green State University Popular Press, 1999).

what he calls the "right wing's loyalty to the classic Western formula."[6]

Conservative columnist Zachary Leeman, writing on the television Western *Hell on Wheels* (2011-2016), praised the series claiming "it's a perfect show for Western lovers and conservatives alike." He went on to praise its portrayal of "manhood," "faith," and service to God. [7] Spencer Warren, writing for the American Conservative Union, writes that the Western is "the most conservative of genres" combating relativism and egalitarianism. [8] Warren specifically points to John Wayne Westerns — Westerns made during the post-war classical period — as the epitome of the Western genre. Michael Talent, writing for the conservative quarterly *Counterpoint*, states "the Western genre of filmmaking … is already inherently right wing,"[9]

The militant anti-communism of the American right wing during the post-war period helped to solidify this relationship with the Western genre. The gunfighter's role in defending the innocent from outlaws served as an analogy for the American state's role in defending the free world from Soviet domination. This was not lost on a generation of Cold-War Americans. Even outside the United States, the imagery

---

[6] Robert B. Ray, *A Certain Tendency of the Hollywood Cinema, 1930-1980.* (Princeton, NJ: Princeton University Press, 1985) p. 351.
[7] Zachary Leeman, "AMC's 'Hell on Wheels' Delivers a Conservative Blast of Western Values," Breitbart.com, Aug 12, 2012,
https://www.breitbart.com/entertainment/2012/08/12/amc-s-hell-on-wheels-deserves-a-hell-of-a-chance/.
[8] Spencer Warren, "John Wayne's First 100 Years," The American Conservative Union Foundation, March 7, 2011,
http://web.archive.org/web/20110307030755/http://www.conservative.org/wp-content/themes/Conservative/bl-archive/Issues/issue87/070707med.php
[9] Michael Talent, "Apolitical Grit," *Counterpoint,* January 12, 2011,
http://counterpoint.uchicago.edu/archives/winter2011/grit.html

was very powerful and was famously used in a poster designed by the Polish Solidarity movement promoting the 1989 election, an election that was a referendum on Communist rule.[10]

The point of bringing up the conservative affinity for Westerns is simply to take note of at least one group of Americans likely to look with favor on what they regard as "traditional" values. Those who look back to an earlier America for insights about what are traditional values are not all political conservatives of course, but in the culture wars that have arisen in the United States since the 1960s, the Western has become something of a lodestar for the proponents of a value system they associate with an earlier American way of life.

But what are these supposedly traditional values? Generally, defenders of the classical Western hold that the genre embodies the values of hard work, private property, family, community, and a Christian (sometimes broadened to "Judeo-Christian") moral framework. These are values historically associated with the nineteenth-century American middle class, and as such, with what one might refer to as "traditional" American society. Even decades after Westerns ceased to dominate the airwaves and movie reels, the way that Western and frontier iconography and idiom has been used by politicians such as Ronald Reagan and George W. Bush speaks to the power of those symbols in harking back to a set of values perceived to be synonymous with traditional American civilization.

In the analysis of the conservative fans of the genre, the classical Western is promoted as an artistic form providing an example of virtuous behavior. This is believed to be most true of Westerns from the post-war classical period, which

---

[10] The poster encouraged Poles to vote in the upcoming election, and used an image of Gary Cooper from *High Noon* holding a ballot.

many people living today may remember from childhood. Additionally, it is often assumed that the Western provides an imitable example that points us toward an admittedly romanticized but desirable way of life involving family and community.

It is difficult to package a complex set of values into a single term, but here I will refer to this set of values as "bourgeois liberal values." This is a heavily-loaded phrase of course, and in Europe during various periods, and among Marxists, the term "bourgeois liberal" might have many different meanings. Indeed, the term is still used today by Marxists and other anti-capitalists as an insult term or epithet designed to denote a corrupt or plutocratic ruling class. In America, however, bourgeois liberalism (using "liberalism" in the historical and classical sense) might also be considered in an unbiased and matter-of-fact way as simply the dominant ideology of the American middle class during the nineteenth century.

Much like its counterpart in increasingly liberal Britain during the nineteenth century, the American middle class was focused on wealth accumulation, private property, industrialization, domestic life, religious devotion, and anti-authoritarian politics. It is during this period that we see the rise of Victorian America, which in many ways mirrors British Victorian society and its values. Due to the lack of an anti-liberal aristocracy in the United States, however, American Victorianism was even more closely associated with middle-class liberalism than was the case in Britain.[11] Victorian

---

[11] The rise of liberalism in the 1830s and 1840s in Britain is widely considered to be closely connected to the Victorian society that came to dominate during the second half of the nineteenth century. Some historians classify capitalist liberal Richard Cobden and his Anti-Corn Law League, and the liberal movement behind it, as an important aspect of the rising Victorian culture. The old conservative aristocracy in Britain, however, opposed the middle classes. Samuel Taylor Coleridge, for example, following the

society is historically marked by significant growth in the middle classes, industrialization, formal education, scientific inquiry, and by the growing influence of women in cultural and literary trends. The political ideology of this period in America was heavily influenced by the classical liberalism of the late eighteenth-century American revolutionaries, and was sustained through art and literature that reiterated the assumed virtues of the "Founding Fathers." These founders were in many cases very wealthy patricians, but were nevertheless revered by the American middle classes.[12]

Connecting the Western to the historical period it purportedly dramatizes, proponents of the classical Western often assume that these nineteenth-century values are the values supported and endorsed by the narratives of the Western film. But are they really?

In this essay I will explore the cultural message of prominent Westerns of the classical period (extending from

---

adoption of the Reform Act of 1832 in Parliament, condemned the act for giving political power to the middle classes and declared that "you have agitated and exasperated the mob, and thrown the balance of political power into the hands of that class which, in all countries and in all ages, has been, is now, and ever will be, the least patriotic and least conservative of any...." Ryan McMaken, "Conservatism," in *Encyclopedia of Modern Political Thought*, ed. Gregory Claeys (Thousand Oaks, CA: CQ Press, 2013). p. 182.

[12] Victorianism, which is specific to the nineteenth century, is not synonymous with classical liberalism, which extends beyond any one time period. However, its close connections with the urban middle classes of the nineteenth century create a historical symbiosis between both movements. One should also note that Victorianism was not exclusive to liberals. Thomas Carlyle in Britain, for example, was anti-liberal and anti-capitalist, but was one of the most influential essayists of the Victorian period. In the United States, however, where liberalism was the dominant ideology, Victorianism was even more associated with liberalism than was the case in Britain.

approximately 1945 to 1965) and contrast classical Westerns with later revisionist Westerns.

Although few watch them today, I will also briefly examine how early silent and B-Westerns differed markedly from what we now consider to be traditional Westerns. Certainly, the films made from the late 1890s through the 1930s were important in the development of the genre, but they exert much less direct influence in modern popular culture and political discourse than the classical Westerns. When politicians and American film audiences think of archetypal Westerns today, they are almost always referring to the Westerns of John Ford and other Westerns of the 1940s, 1950s and 1960s. It is the values of the classical Western that are still closely associated with the genre as a whole. This value system is generally supposed to reflect bourgeois liberal, and thus solid middle-class ideologies, but an examination of films like *High Noon* (1952), *Rio Bravo* (1959), and *She Wore a Yellow Ribbon* (1949), suggest that an altogether different set of values is being put forward by the classical Western.

Ironically, the post-classical revisionist Westerns, such as the works of Sergio Leone and Clint Eastwood, often derided as being opposed to these bourgeois values, are more sympathetic to such values than are the classical Westerns, and they resemble older pre-classical Westerns in some of their pro-Indian and anti-authoritarian themes.

The structure and content of the classical Western genre is largely incompatible with the bourgeois liberal values of the Americans who actually lived during the historical period depicted within the films themselves. The extent of this incompatibility varies over time, but is evident in the fact that the most popular literary forms of the mid- and late-nineteenth century were very different in form and content from the Western genre. As Jane Tompkins contends in *West of Everything*, the Western as a genre is in many ways a revolt against the dominant culture of the Victorians and is a rejection of the domestic and religious environment that accompanied the rise of liberalism and industrialization.[13] Ann Douglas also explores this theme in *Terrible Honesty* and *The Feminization of American Culture*.[14] In the works of Tompkins and Douglas, we find that the literary and artistic conventions of the twentieth century, the Western among them, attempt to do away with the assumptions and characteristics of the nineteenth-century Victorian literature which largely mirrors middle-class bourgeois values of the nineteenth century.

Central to the narrative of the classical Western is the assumption that the frontier was uncommonly violent, and that Victorian bourgeois values were unsuited to such a harsh landscape. In the Western genre's typical narrative, bourgeois middle-class values would eventually be established on the frontier, but only after the gunfighter successfully tamed the land. The imagery of the violent frontier would prove to be immensely successful in de-valuing the bourgeois lifestyle which in the Western genre is incapable of sustaining itself without the intervention of a sheriff or a cavalryman or a semi-feral gunman.

In recent decades, historians have challenged this view of the violent American frontier, and I will examine the level of true violence that existed on the real frontier and how it differs from the image offered by the Western.

Finally, I will look at one form of the Western that actually does reflect the liberal bourgeois values that all Westerns supposedly endorse: the *Little House on the Prairie* (1974-1983) television series. It can be argued, however, that

---

[13] Jane Tompkins. *West of Everything: The Inner Life of Westerns*, (Oxford: Oxford University Press. 1993), p. 55.
[14] Ann Douglas, *The Feminization of American Culture*, New York, NY: Farrar, Straus and Giroux, 1977), and Ann Douglas, *Terrible Honesty: Mongrel Manhattan in the 1920s*, (New York, NY: Farrar, Straus and Giroux, 1995).

the Little House series is not part of the Western genre at all. It lacks any gunfighter as a central character and it is far less violent than the typical Western television show or feature film of the post-war period. With its emphasis on family, schooling, women, and domestic life, the series in many ways rejects the conventional Western in favor of a system of values for which the classical Western narrative has little room.

Influential scholars of the Western like John Cawelti and Richard Etulain have long sought to specifically define the Western and what sets it apart from other genres.[15] It is not enough that a storyline take place on a frontier location to make it a Western. Willa Cather's novel *O Pioneers!*, for example, is rarely considered to be a Western although it takes place on the frontier. A similar, although rarely-asserted, argument might be made about Howard Hawks' *The Furies* (1950), which could be described as a family drama that happens to take place in a frontier setting. Whether a Western or not, the immensely popular *Little House* series, by offering a contrasting vision, helps illustrate how the classical Western embraces a much different value system than what many of its proponents think it does.

Other elements that are often considered essential to the genre include an arid landscape, a setting in "cattle country," and a specific time frame restricted to the period between the end of the Civil War and the official closing of the frontier in the 1890s.

Any casual survey of the early silent Western films would illustrate that Westerns have not, in fact, always taken place in

---

[15] John Lenihan, *Showdown: Confronting Modern America in the Western Film,* (Urbana, IL: University of Illinois Press, 1980), p. 18-22. How the Western is defined depends has been a topic of contention among numerous scholars. In this essay, I have chosen to simply employ the more popular Westerns or those made by the more influential directors.

arid climates, in cattle country, or during such a limited time period. Historically, Westerns have included ante-bellum wagon train dramas and adventure stories of the early nineteenth century. Many early Westerns also used tales from James Fenimore Cooper's Leatherstocking series, which took place during the eighteenth century. Often the settings of these early films were in heavily wooded areas and in riparian landscapes that would be extremely rare among the classical Westerns of the post-World War II period. Indeed, to restrict Westerns to only the deserts and high plains, one would have to necessarily exclude most Westerns about Jesse James for example, or any films featuring mountain landscapes such as *The Naked Spur* (1953).

The fact that Westerns are so closely associated with cattle drives and desert landscapes, however, illustrates the almost hegemonic influence of the classical Western over all other variations of the genre. From the 1940s to the 1960s, Westerns would become nearly synonymous with cactus, tumbleweeds, Apaches, and cattle barons.

The classical Western themes and settings are typified in the films of three directors. During the 1940s and 50s, as the Western grew to the height of its popularity, three of the most influential and popular directors of Westerns were John Ford, Anthony Mann, and Howard Hawks. These men helped develop the Western film into the iconic genre we know today, and they dominated Western films for decades with their epic and influential big-budget Westerns. Films like *Fort Apache* (1948), *Winchester '73* (1950), and *Rio Bravo* (1957) are considered defining films in the history of the Western, and in these films and others by these directors the canon of the classical Western took shape.

Later revisionist Westerns also provide additional insights into how the Western can evolve over time. Sergio Leone, Sam Peckinpah, and Clint Eastwood revolutionized the Western in the 1960s and 70s. In fact, before the traditional Western had even disappeared, Leone and Peckinpah were reworking it and questioning many of the

11

original themes and conclusions. The later Westerns could be critical of the classical Westerns, but they, with a few exceptions, never totally abandoned the themes set out from the earliest days of the genre.

The Gunfighter vs. Classical Liberalism

In analysis from Marxist historians like Eric Hobsbawm to classical-liberal historians like Paul Gottfried, the political liberalism that dominated the nineteenth century was so closely tied to the rise of the bourgeois middle class as to be virtually inseparable.[16] As Gottfried describes it in *After Liberalism*, the old classical liberalism of the nineteenth century was centered on the values of the rising middle class that glorified the business-oriented private property owner.[17] These middle class liberals valued self-responsibility, a commitment to family, and an acceptance of long-term obligations to both home and the workplace. The "good" man of the nineteenth-century middle class planned for the future with sound savings and investment. He was a part of the complex economic and social systems of families, markets, and political institutions, all of which he used to forward bourgeois goals. He was also, for the most part, a religious man.

Liberalism dominated politics throughout America and Western Europe at various times during the eighteenth and nineteenth centuries as members of the rising bourgeois classes, chafing under the yoke of ancient systems of government privilege and control, set out to gain access to power. In place of the old regimes, the bourgeoisie wanted nation-states friendly toward free trade, low taxes, large-scale

---

[16] Eric Hobsbawm, *The Age of Capital: 1848-1875* (London: Vintage Books, 1996), pp. 230-250.

[17] Paul Gottfried, *After Liberalism: Mass Democracy in the Managerial State* (Princeton, NJ: Princeton University Press, 2001), p. 35.

business enterprises, and political liberty. And they wanted peace. When one is the owner of a major economic enterprise dependent on international trade, unless one is politically well connected, war can be extremely bad for business. The American wars that were fought in this period, such as the wars with Native Americans and with the Mexicans, were justified on the grounds that they would eliminate the need for wars in the future.

The aversion to war had been obvious among American liberals from the late eighteenth century. Writing in 1795, the former American revolutionary James Madison concluded that

> Of all enemies to public liberty, war is, perhaps, the most to be dreaded, because it comprises and develops the germ of every other. War is the parent of armies; from these proceed debts and taxes; and armies, and debts, and taxes are the known instruments for bringing the many under the domination of the few.[18]

Referring to Madison's view on war, historian Ralph Raico writes:

> This was the position not only of Washington and Madison, but of John Adams, Thomas Jefferson, and the other men who presided over the birth of the United States. For over a century, it was adhered to and elaborated by our leading statesmen. It could be called neutrality, or nonintervention, or America

---

[18] James Madison, *Letters and Other Writings of James Madison Vol. IV* (Philadelphia: J.B. Lippincott & Co., 1865), 491.
http://archive.org/stream/lettersandotherw04madiiala#page/490/mode/2up

first, or, as its modern enemies dubbed it, isolationism.[19]

There were always some proponents of aggressive warfare of course, as with Henry Clay and his nationalists. Nevertheless, the influence of the early American liberals, given their stature in American political discourse, extended nearly to the end of the nineteenth century.

In Britain, the corresponding anti-war position of Richard Cobden and his Manchester liberals further reinforced the relationship between the Victorian-era bourgeois liberalism and a preference for commerce over violence.

The bourgeoisie were naturally criticized for this aversion to war. In the nascent days of liberal dominance in Britain, Napoleon Bonaparte is said to have scoffed at the British as a nation of shopkeepers, concerned with matters of commerce when they should have been tending to more glorious pursuits such as war.[20] Some critical Brits theorized that their countrymen, the Manchester liberals, would gladly have accepted military conquest by the French, as long as it produced new business opportunities. In America, Victorian-era exemplars of liberalism, men like Edward Atkinson,

---

[19] Ralph Raico, "American Foreign Policy — The Turning Point, 1898–1919," April 1, 1995, Future of Freedom Foundation, https://www.fff.org/explore-freedom/article/american-foreign-policy-turning-point-18981919-part-1/

[20] Ralph Raico, "Eugen Richter and Late German Manchester Liberalism," *The Review of Austrian Economics*, 4 (1990): 3-25. Raico describes how the German conservatives of the nineteenth century opposed the liberals in a variety of ways. "Manchester liberalism," the liberalism associated with Richard Cobden and *laissez faire* capitalism, especially won disdain from Otto von Bismarck who contemptuously referred to "Manchester money-bags" for Manchesterism's support of free trade and free markets, and for its connection to the newly wealthy middle classes.

founder of the Anti-Imperialist League, and William Graham Sumner, were seen as excessively attached to peace and free trade and were denounced as seditious.[21] Writing on Sumner's 1899 condemnation of the Spanish-American War, Raico notes that the time-honored game of international intrigue and victory on the battlefield was indeed the way of the great powers. But, according to Sumner

> it was not the *American* way. That way had been more modest, more prosaic, parochial, and, yes, *middle class*. It was based on the idea that we were here to live out our lives, minding our own business, enjoying our liberty, and pursuing our happiness in our work, families, churches, and communities. It had been the "small policy."[22]

This apparent liberal pre-occupation with the economic sphere has been linked historically with liberalism since its early years in the writings of John Locke. Locke, considered to be one of the earliest liberal theorists, was key in fashioning the importance of private property and its protection as a central component of liberal ideology. For Locke, the acquisition of private property exists in the state of nature, and the cultivation and protection of wealth is one of

---

[21] Not surprisingly, Sumner and Atkinson were both patrician types of the Northeastern United States which culturally dominated during the Victorian period in the United States. Both were part of the laissez-faire, anti-war school of American liberalism during the late nineteenth century. Atkinson famously authored a pamphlet calling for American soldiers to mutiny against their officers and to refuse to fight the Filipinos during the American occupation of that country. Copies of the pamphlet were seized by the United States government.

[22] Ralph Raico, "American Foreign Policy — The Turning Point, 1898–1919,"

the foundational elements behind the formation and perpetuation of human society.

Key to Locke's philosophy, and of particular importance to an evaluation of the Western genre in relation to liberalism, is the fact that Locke accepted that order in society was obtainable without the interference of a state apparatus. While Locke can accept the presence of a limited state apparatus in securing pre-existing property rights, societal order itself precedes the state and as such is not based on coercive power.

As literary critic Paul Cantor notes in his analysis of *Deadwood*, "Locke can imagine an economic order independent of the political order,"[23] and this proves to be important in our evaluation of the genre in which the gunfighter is so often a figure analogous to political power.

The Western stands contrary to the liberal emphasis on both peace and commerce. As we shall see, the chief narrative behind the classical Western is that the spread of civilization and economic prosperity is not possible without the presence of a nation-state apparatus or at least a state-like apparatus in the form of the gunfighter. The gunfighter, like states themselves, employs coercive and war-like force to mete out punishment and to gain compliance, and this is portrayed as the foundational act of civilization. Eventually, this narrative met with enthusiastic acceptance from millions of Americans for whom the Second World War and the Cold War were defining events in their lives.

The necessity of violence in making civilization possible is especially evident in the cavalry sub-genre of the Western. In *She Wore a Yellow Ribbon* (1949), the narrator in the film's prologue informs the viewer that "one more such defeat as

___

[23] Paul A. Cantor, "Order out of the Mud," in *The Philosophy of the Western.* (Lexington, KY: University Press of Kentucky, 2010), p. 121.

Custer's and it would be a hundred years before another wagon train dared to cross the plains."

Historically speaking, this statement almost comically exaggerates the threat that the Native Americans posed to the Westward expansion of whites. Even without this hyperbole, however, *She Wore a Yellow Ribbon* and John Ford's other cavalry films, *Fort Apache* and *Rio Grande* (1950), all assume that the role of the cavalry is to pave the way for civilization on the frontier. The option of co-existence between the whites and the Indians in these films is assumed to be unworthy of even the most terse discussion. The classical Westerns assume that any solution involving the Indians and the whites living near each other would result in a state of total warfare. The only option then, is total removal or eradication of the Indians, made possible by a strong United States cavalry.

The role of the cavalry in ushering in civilization is also presented symbolically in John Ford's *Stagecoach* (1939) in which the passengers of the stagecoach are only able to obtain safe passage through the frontier via the intervention of the United States cavalry. The stagecoach, America in microcosm, attempts to cross the hazardous wilds, and is finally escorted safely to its destination. The heroes of the film, who would have been massacred had it not been for the cavalry, are then able to get on with the business of building civilization.

On a smaller scale, in *Winchester '73*, the only reason peaceful city life is possible in Dodge City is because the town's sheriff, Wyatt Earp, has instituted a draconian policy of gun control in which no one but official law enforcement officers are permitted to carry guns within city limits. Outside the town, where no official law enforcement exists, the main characters are subject to murderous Indians, unscrupulous businessmen, and a perpetual state of war.

This choice between a war of all against all, and a government strong enough to eradicate the Indians and confiscate firearms, is a frequent theme in Westerns and places the gunfighter (in these cases a cavalryman or sheriff) at the center of civilized life. Although John Locke may have been able to imagine a functioning society that existed before government, the Western film clearly cannot.

In contrast to the coercive power of the gunman in film are the concerns of the typical middle-class American of the real-life frontier period. With liberalism as the primary political ideology in America, private commercial and domestic concerns were of chief importance. The middle-class bourgeois cultural mores that accompanied this ideology were equally important on the historical frontier. Dignity, restraint, prudence, thrift, and practical commercial skills were viewed as important values that provided a solid foundation for the preservation and advancement of Christian civilization. The role of self-defense by force was certainly not ignored, but it was not given primacy above all other skills.

Indeed, one of the most notable characteristics of classical liberalism was its departure from medieval societal norms that placed soldiering and war-making at the summit of human societal values. In some of the wealthiest and most liberal societies, such as in the Dutch Republic, the image of the patrician or aristocrat as soldier and military hero had been replaced by the image of patricians who were businessmen or bureaucrats dressed in sensible black clothes as in Rembrandt's iconic painting "The Syndics of the Drapers' Guild."

In the real-life settlements of the American West, the settlers carried this liberal civilization to a new frontier. Back in the East, the older agricultural way of life was giving way to the new urban way of life, and many Americans found themselves working in factories instead of on farms and living in cities instead of small towns. Wealthier Americans began moving to the first suburbs, and railroads made travel available to most middle-class Americans. Early factory life and urban living enjoys a negative reputation among many today, but for the Victorians, these developments were a sign of progress and the spread of civilization.

The gunfighter in film, however, whether wandering loner, sheriff, or military man, is not part of this Victorian liberal world, and is very rarely a member of the bourgeoisie or part of a bourgeois family structure. Very few of the protagonists from Westerns of the classical period are businessmen or family men. Most are cavalry officers, sheriffs or marshals, although Anthony Mann's protagonists are often small-time proprietors in the form of bounty hunters and guns for hire. Even the few Western protagonists with children, such as Tom Dunson (John Wayne) in *Red River* (1948), are unmarried or estranged from their wives; and among television Westerns, which tended to be more family-themed, patriarch Ben Cartwright of *Bonanza* (1959-1973) and Lucas McCain of *The Rifleman* (1958-1963), for example, are both widowers.

Typically, the gunfighter does not own property of any consequence, and he does not have savings or make investments. He rarely has a family, and he rarely has any use for religion at all. In the Western, this figure so contrary to bourgeois sensibilities remains always at the center of the action. There might be a businessman or family patriarch somewhere in the background, but such figures remain more or less as props viewing the action with little more input than the audience sitting in the theatre. More often than not, businessmen are villains.[24]

The classical Western centers not on bourgeois values of commerce and hearth and home, but on martial values of physical courage, skill with weaponry, and power through violence. Perhaps there is nothing to dislike about things such as courage and skill in battle. Yet what we find in the classical

---

[24] There are exceptions, of course, as in *3:10 to Yuma* (1957) in which family-man Dan Evans is the heroic protagonist, but the model of an unattached gunman as hero is far more common.

Western is that these values, as personified in the gunfighter, are not complementary values to the bourgeois world, but generally are in conflict with it. Through its literary conventions, the Western turns the value system of the historical frontier on its head.

In the classical Western, bourgeois liberal values are viewed not just as irrelevant to the final resolution of the plot, but are portrayed as a hindrance to the neutralization and punishment of the villains. What is essential to the proper resolution of conflicts in the Western is the frequent application of deadly force upon both the white and Indian residents of the frontier.

Violence and Profit on the Frontier

In a typical storyline from the classical Western, the bourgeois society of the town must subject itself to the authority of the gunfighter or face annihilation. The choice that faces the townsfolk is to either accept the supremacy of the gunfighter, who personifies the state in the classical Western, or to accept oppression at the hands of Indians, outlaws, or worse. Self-defense provided by the community itself is rarely an option, nor would it be sufficient. For the bourgeois settlers, consumed by their petty commercial and domestic pursuits, little can be done except to meekly submit to superior physical force.

To establish ideal conditions for the extension of the fable, the classical Western makes two assertions that are central to the life of the genre. First, it creates the image of an American West that is extremely violent. Second, the genre requires that the residents of the frontier be incapable of defending themselves so that they may only be saved after they abandon their naïve bourgeois ways and embrace militarism and gunfights as their only hope in avoiding destruction.

This image of the historical frontier was challenged little during the years of the classical Western, but since the 1970s, there has been a growing body of research debunking the image of the bloody and Wild West. In spite of this, the power of the Western genre in the minds of Americans has proven its staying power. The myth of the Wild West remains.

In their 1979 study on Western violence, Terry Anderson and P.J. Hill write that

> The taste for the dramatic in literature and other entertainment forms has led to concentration on the seeming disparity between the Westerners' desire for order and the prevailing disorder. If the Hollywood image of the West were not enough to taint our view, scholars of violence have contributed with quotes such as the following: "We can report with some assurance that compared to frontier days there has been a significant decrease in crimes of violence in the United States."

> Recently, however, more careful examinations of the conditions that existed cause one to doubt the accuracy of this perception. In his book, *Frontier Violence: Another Look*, W. Eugene Hollon stated that he believed "that the Western frontier was a far more civilized, more peaceful, and safer place than American society is today." The legend of the "wild, wild West" lives on despite Robert Dykstra's finding that in five of the major cattle towns (Abilene, Ellsworth, Wichita, Dodge City, and Caldwell) for the years from 1870 to 1885, only 45 homicides were reported—an average of 1.5 per cattle-trading season.

> In Abilene, supposedly one of the wildest of the cow towns, "nobody was killed in 1869 or 1870. In fact, nobody was killed until the advent of officers of the law, employed to prevent killings." Only two towns, Ellsworth in 1873 and Dodge City in 1876, ever had 5 killings in any one year. Frank Prassel

states in his book subtitled *A Legacy of Law and Order*, that "if any conclusion can be drawn from recent crime statistics, it must be that this last frontier left no significant heritage of offenses against the person, relative to other sections of the country."[25]

Modern perceptions of violence on the frontier are so shaped by the fictional accounts from the Western genre that they are nearly impossible for many people to distinguish from the actual historical facts about the frontier.

Historian Richard Shenkman noted "Many more people have died [i.e., been murdered] in Hollywood Westerns than ever died on the real frontier."[26] As summarized by Jodi McEndarfer,[27] the work of historians like Robert Dykstra and Richard Brown tends to leave one underwhelmed as to the magnitude of frontier violence. For example, while the Kansas code gave mayors the power to call a vigilante group from all the men in the town who ranged in ages from 18–50, it seems, at least in Kansas, that it was rare.[28] Over 38 years, Kansas had only 19 vigilante movements that accounted for

---

[25] Terry L. Anderson and P.J. Hill, "An American Experiment in Anarcho-Capitalism: The Not So Wild, Wild West," *Journal of Libertarian Studies*, 3, no. 1 (1979): 14.
https://mises.org/library/american-experiment-anarcho-capitalism-not-so-wild-wild-west.
[26] Richard Shenkman, *Legends, Lies, and Cherished Myths of American History*, (New York: Morrow, 1988), p. 112.
[27] Jodi McEndarfer, "Violence in the Cattle Towns," Indiana University, 2001,
https://scholarworks.iu.edu/journals/index.php/iusburj/article/download/19835/25912/43972.
[28] Dykstra, Robert R. *The Cattle Towns*. (Lincoln, NE: The University of Nebraska Press, 1983), p. 116.

18 deaths.[29] In addition, between 1876 and 1886, no one was lynched or hanged illegally in Dodge City.[30] Deadwood, South Dakota and Tombstone, Arizona (home of the O.K. Corral), during their worst years of violence saw four and five murders respectively. Vigilante violence appears not to have been much worse.

Given the money to be made by exploiting the exciting reputation of the frontier, it is not surprising that Dodge City was hardly alone in manufacturing tales of blazing guns to attract men seeking adventure. Towns like Tombstone, Abilene, and Deadwood all played up their supposed histories of frontier violence. On closer inspection though, the records are not nearly as exciting.

If the movies and novels about the West are unreliable, what can we learn from documented cases about real life violence in the West? Certainly, a case that resembles the quintessential blood feud in the West would be the Lincoln County war of 1878–81, which largely made the reputation of notorious gunfighter Billy the Kid. As the name of the "war" implies, this unpleasantness was quite disruptive to southern New Mexico, and produced quite its share of dead bodies. But even then, we find a body count intolerably low by Hollywood standards.

When the smoke cleared from this unusually violent conflagration, the legend remains far more violent than the reality. After all, authorities have only been able to prove that Billy the Kid, generally regarded as the most blood-soaked participant in the Lincoln County War, killed three people. Most agree that he may possibly have killed as many as three or four more people, but considering the circumstances, it is

---

[29] Richard Maxwell Brown, *Strain of Violence: Historical Studies of American Violence and Vigilantism* (New York, NY: Oxford University Press, 1975), p. 311.

[30] Elliott West, "Wicked Dodge City," *American History Illustrated*, 17 no.4 (1982): 22-31.

difficult to ascertain how The Kid managed to gain a reputation as a psychopathic killer or how stories began to circulate of how he had killed 21 men by the time he was 21. Much of the confusion was due, as Shenkman indicates, to American movies. Films like *Chisum* (1970), which portrays Billy as a rather sympathetic character, and *Young Guns* (1988), which makes Billy look a bit more crazy, play up the violence of the Lincoln County War for obvious reasons. However, even considering the rather alarming body count (by contemporary as well as modern standards), events like the Lincoln County War were hardly everyday occurrences.

The existence of a real-life frontier where a wandering gunfighter is not actually needed is something that needs to be ignored in the world of the Western genre. In real life, one of the remarkable characteristics of the frontier is that it was more or less self-policing. In most cases, it was little more than a loose confederation of municipalities and local governments held together only by economic interests. National pride consisted of little more than a loyalty to a far-off national government that in the early days of the frontier was virtually invisible, and even in later times was still represented by only small and rarely-seen bands of cavalry. In other words, it was a society where political power was locally controlled, economic dealings were virtually unregulated, and defense of an individual's property was usually the responsibility of the individual.

The frontier was a place where people went to make money, and they stayed there if they made it. If they failed, they returned to the East. Certainly, many people died unpleasant deaths on the frontier from disease, accidents, and general misfortune, but such things were sure to befall travelers undertaking similar endeavors anywhere in the world in the nineteenth century.

The truly important question is whether or not human beings on the frontier were less prosperous, more violent, and generally more barbaric than their counterparts in more "civilized" parts of the world. If this can be proven to be the case, then the case for active government, commercial regulation, and an aggressive police apparatus is granted much more currency in the minds of Americans. Not surprisingly, the classical Western film became a useful tool in promoting an active and interventionist government in post-World War II America. If the intervention of a well-trained cavalry and a steady-handed sheriff were what made civilization possible on the frontier, then the same could be justified on a global scale during the mid-twentieth century or today.

In reality, the settling of the American frontier represents some of the most undirected, spontaneous and free settling of land seen since the ancient world. All modern frontier states (i.e., Australia, Canada, and the Latin American countries) were settled for largely economic reasons by settlers willing to brave an unknown geography, but nowhere was the state less involved in this settlement than on the American frontier.

For example, the wagon train phenomenon so closely identified with the settlement of the West, was largely started in the early 1840s by the Mormons fleeing religious persecution in the settled United States. They enjoyed little protection from U.S. marshals or cavalry. Once on the frontier, the Mormons quickly set up shop in their new environs and began trading with both the Americans in the east and with the Mexican settlers on the West Coast (as well as Indians). While many other Americans began to brave the plains to travel to the riches described in the guidebooks about Oregon and California, the trend only began to really accelerate after the discovery of gold in California in 1849. By 1850, there were thousands of wagon trains on the trail to California with one train rarely out of sight of another.[31]

---

[31] Louis L'amour, *Showdown Trail*. (New York, NY: Bantam Audio Publishing, 1987). In this edition, L'amour provides an introduction in which he discusses the nature of wagon-train life.

The wagon trains created a large mobile economic system that moved across the plains. Entire industries grew up around getting people to their destinations and serving them once they got there. Scouts, guides, equipment, guidebooks and teamsters were all readily supplied by enthusiastic entrepreneurs. Wagons and families moved from one train to another as conditions and preferences dictated. This image, of course, is in contrast to the movie version of the wagon train experience in which one wagon train moves alone and isolated across the plains and is subject to Indian raids and outlaws with nowhere to look for help but the steady hand of the gunfighter.

In fact, as Louis L'amour has noted, many wagon trains of the day had been organized like small private armies, complete with embroidered uniforms that resembled "an army detachment."[32] These steps were made to ensure self-sufficiency in private law enforcement, but on a day-to-day basis, what concerned these settlers most was not law enforcement or gunfights with hostile Indians. Far more pressing were the problems of obtaining food and other resources, educating children, enjoying some leisure time, and making money. One would hardly get this impression from a Hollywood Western.

Often, the model of the frontier settler that suits the myth-maker is the model of the settler-as-victim. This has been quite popular in novels and in film simply for its versatility as a plot device, but it sends a clear message. Anthony Mann's *The Tin Star* (1957), for example, features a town of gullible settlers easily led astray by a resident outlaw, and who are best ruled by a sheriff with an iron fist. In *Shane*, the settlers are incapable of defending themselves until a wandering gunfighter selflessly provides the protection they need. This plot device persists even into early revisionist Westerns such as Sergio Leone's *A Fistful of Dollars* (1964) in

---

[32] *Ibid.*

which the Man with No Name stumbles upon a terrorized village and proceeds to eliminate crime from the town with a fast gun and a Machiavellian mind.

Probably most notable in the defenseless-villager sub genre, however, is *High Noon* (1952) with Gary Cooper fruitlessly attempting to recruit a posse to beat back invading outlaws. By the end of the film, Marshal Will Kane (Cooper), disgusted with the lack of courage in the town, tosses his star into the dust of the frontier town "too dishonorable to deserve protection."[33]

As film historian Thomas Doherty notes, the "slanderous central conceit" of *High Noon* was that "the Old West was packed with no-account yellow-bellies."[34] Notably, the cowardly townspeople are concerned about real-estate values and boring old business matters rather than with settling scores with the bad guys. The government marshal is heroic. The local merchants are cowards.

The Western repeatedly sets up a tale of gunfighters (themselves almost supernatural in their wisdom and invincibility) who are beyond the comprehension of ordinary polite society. The gunfighter serves a near-messianic role on the frontier as he saves the bewildered townspeople from their enemies, pulls them away from their petty bourgeois concerns, and unifies them in a struggle against evil.

Unfortunately for any Hollywood scriptwriter aiming for historical accuracy, the American West was far less exciting than the Westerns would lead people to believe. The frontiersmen knew this themselves. In his old age, Buffalo Bill Cody, one of the most flamboyant architects of our perceptions of the West, openly admitted to lying about his

---

[33] Thomas Doherty, "Western Drama, Cold-War Allegory." In *The Chronicle of Higher Education*. September 13, 2002.
http://archives.econ.utah.edu/archives/marxism/2002w37/msg00
058.html
[34] *Ibid.*

violent exploits to sell more dime novels. He was, after all, wounded in battle with Indians exactly once, not the 137 times he claimed.[35] Such tales were also immensely popular with Americans of the mid-twentieth century who seemed open to believing almost anything about the West as long as it was simultaneously exciting and violent.

Kit Carson, one of the earliest heroes of the proto-Western literature of the mid-nineteenth century, was troubled late in life by the image many had of him as a frontier hero:

> In 1849, Kit Carson was searching through New Mexico for a white woman taken captive by the Jicarilla Apaches, a certain Mrs. J. M. White. Locating their camp, he noticed among the debris an abandoned book, which turned out to be a novel about the scouting exploits of Kit Carson, probably one published the same year titled *Kit Carson: Prince of the Gold Hunters*. As it happened, the real Carson could not match the skills of his fictional double, and Mrs. White was found dead. He long remained troubled by the thought that she must have been given hope in her captivity by reading this Western "in which I was made a great hero, slaying Indians by the hundred."[36]

One can argue, as has conservative columnist Gary North, that the violence of the Western is nothing more than harmless attempts to capitalize on public thirst for adventure

[35] Richard Zacks, *An Underground Education* (New York, NY: Anchor Books, 1997), p. 381.
[36] Scott Simmon, *The Invention of the Western Film: A Cultural History of the Genre's First Half Century* (Cambridge, UK: Cambridge University Press, 2003), p. xi.

and excitement in cinema.[37] There is no doubt that the popularity of the Western genre during the first half of the twentieth century, and its popularity in the form of the dime novels during the nineteenth century, is at least partially explained by its violent content.

As Engelhardt has shown in *The End of Victory Culture*, however, the classical Western at mid-century became important as a mechanism for reinforcing American perceptions about the need for the use of military force and the helplessness of civilian populations in the face of menacing foreign enemies. Although the treatment of civilian "polite" society and violence was often more complex and less absolutist in early silent Westerns, the fact that earlier Western source material set the stage for the myth of the ultra-violent frontier enabled later makers of the classical Western to enhance both gunfighter violence and villager impotence. The sheer volume and repetitiveness of this message in classical Westerns during the 1940s and 50s would help make the Western into an important vehicle for reflecting and reinforcing American sentiments during the Cold War.

Additionally, the Western played a key role in perpetuating inaccurate stereotypes about the American frontier and its viability as a society unregulated by civil government. As noted by Anderson, Hill, and Shenkman, the Western is largely to be blamed for American misperceptions about violence on the frontier, which in turn have been used to argue that American settlements lacking the imposed order of a central government have been uncommonly violent.

---

[37] Gary North, "In Defense of the Classic Western," LewRockwell.com, October 28, 2005, https://www.lewrockwell.com/2005/10/gary-north/in-defense-of-the-classic-western/. North appears to take the position that popular culture doesn't matter in forming the perceptions and ideologies of viewers.

The Gunfighter vs. Capitalism

A recurring theme in the Western is a distrust of industrialized societies and complex economic systems. As Tompkins suggests, just as language is to be distrusted because of its symbolic nature in a sophisticated society, money, as a representation of economic value, is also to be distrusted in the Western.[38] Contracts, bank notes, and deeds are all symbols of economic value that cannot immediately be understood with the physical senses and are therefore suspect. Large businesses in the Western are particularly threatening. Everywhere in the Western, the railroads are a sign of Eastern decadence and corruption. Large ranchers and industrialists commonly attempt to exploit the honest people of the West, and private companies are portrayed as vultures preying on the new settlers.

One of the commonly known examples of this is George Stevens's *Shane* (1953) in which a number of small farmers move onto land that has been run for years by Ryker, the proprietor of a vast cattle ranch. The film's central assumption is that the farmers have a right to Ryker's land for a reason that is left unexplained in the film, except to note that Ryker is motivated by greed. When Ryker objects to the farmers' squatting, he is portrayed as a villain. The film doesn't provide a convincing explanation as to why, exactly, Ryker should give up his land to the farmers. Since the farmers are small underdogs and Ryker is a big rancher, however, he is assumed to be in the wrong.[39] A similar

---

[38] Tompkins, *West of Everything, p 38.*

[39] Ryker is probably a free-range rancher on federal lands, and the farmers are homesteaders. There is no reason to assume that the typical audience member watching films using Shane's central plot device would know the economic history behind them, however, and the films fail to explain things in these terms.

conflict appears in *The Man Who Shot Liberty Valance* (1962), in which the big ranchers oppose statehood and a central government for the territory because it would break their stranglehold on land in the region. The small ranchers are victorious, though, once nationalist sensibilities and democracy are brought to the territory and the fiendish big ranchers are defeated.

In *Rio Bravo*, after a wealthy land baron's brother is jailed, the baron hires a gang of killers to overrun the sheriff's office where the protectors of the honest townsfolk are holed up. *El Dorado* (a 1966 remake of *Rio Bravo*,) naturally employs a very similar plot device. In Anthony Mann's Westerns, new settlers to the West are constantly in danger of conniving businessmen seeking to exploit and defraud anyone who comes into their territory. How exactly these exploiters manage to stay in business is never explained. Yet, in both *The Far Country* (1954) and *Bend of the River* (1952), the central threat to the townsfolk is the local large businessman who is responsible for the corruption of law and order, while Hawks's *The Big Sky* (1952) features an evil fur company that attempts to violently crush all competition. In Mann's *The Man from Laramie* (1955) the local cattle baron not only rules the local town of Coronado with an iron fist, but also collaborates with hostile Indians who threaten the very existence of the town.

These story lines all follow a basic pattern in which the townsfolk are threatened by an aggressive and evil business that seeks to exploit all for its own interests. The only thing standing between these businessmen and their sinister aims is the gunfighter, who is often a government agent, perhaps a sheriff, cavalryman, or a federal marshal. Sometimes, the people beg for deliverance from their capitalist oppressors, as in *Shane*, and sometimes they are oblivious to the true extent and severity of the threat posed, as the settlers are in *The Man from Laramie*.

Private property is certainly a theme in Westerns, but "property rights" is understood as the crushing of large business enterprises for the good of "the people." The view of business in the Western is the view one would expect from a genre that reached its greatest popularity among a population that overwhelmingly supported the New Deal. Everywhere large business interests are out to crush small business interests and must be neutralized. An aversion to the complexities of industrialized bourgeois life is again apparent as simple one-man operations are looked upon with great fondness in the Western, but large enterprises and sophisticated business practices are not to be tolerated.

The Western takes a dim view of the free market in other ways. *Stagecoach* (1939) features a banker stealing the payroll owed to the workers, a particularly insidious act of theft. The banker then proceeds to extol the virtues of the American business class. His hypocrisy is obvious.

Not even small businessmen are safe from the Western's anti-commerce views. *Winchester '73*, *Fort Apache*, and *She Wore a Yellow Ribbon* all feature small-scale merchants who engage in the apparently unforgivable act of attempting to trade guns and other goods with the Indians. Indeed, in *Fort Apache* and *Yellow Ribbon*, a central purpose of the cavalry is to enforce trade embargoes against the Indians. In *Yellow Ribbon*, *The Man from Laramie*, and *Winchester '73*, the merchants are murdered by the very Indians with whom they are trying to do business. Why the Indians would kill those who supply them with essential goods is not explained, but the message to the audience is clear. Such are the wages of trading with the enemy. In *The Man from Laramie*, it is revealed that the villain plans to sell rifles to the local Indians in an effort to keep the Army away so he can rule the entire countryside with an iron fist. One member of the town, upon hearing of the plot, declares "some people will sell anything to make a profit."

The contest between large and small property-owners is dramatized in *Red River* in which settler Tom Dunson builds a small cattle empire in the grasslands of Texas. Before he can begin his herd, however, he must confront the Mexican Don who owns the land. In a showdown with one of the Don's gunmen, Dunson and his assistant learn that the Don lives hundreds of miles away, presumably at the other end of a vast estate. "That's too much land for one man," Dunson's assistant declares. "It ain't decent." Moments later, Dunson shoots and kills the Don's gunman, apparently settling the property dispute permanently.

Dunson proceeds to squat on the Don's land, and the issue of ownership never comes up again. The complexities of land ownership in the American borderlands are reduced to the simplistic notion that the Don had "too much land for one man" and that he presumably "took it from someone else" first.

As a business owner, even Dunson inevitably becomes a villain as his commitment to drive his cattle from Texas to Kansas slowly turns into violent megalomania. Dunson begins murdering any employee who expresses doubts about the venture when things begin to go poorly.

Given the Western's origins, there is nothing surprising about its anti-capitalist stand against the nineteenth century and all its factories, corporations, stock markets and other components of an economically advanced civilization. In the Western, it is alright to do business, but not too much business lest one become corrupted. Contrary to the nineteenth-century bourgeois liberals who saw free trade and markets as a source of enduring prosperity, peace, and cooperation, the Western sees business and trade as a zero-sum game where exploitation is much more likely than cooperation.

Free-market defenders of the Western have argued that although the Western seems to portray businessmen in a bad light, the genre is really showing a conflict between truly private business interests and politically influential corporatists in league with government officials.[40] North, for

---

[40] North, "In Defense of the Classic Western."

example, bases this claim on the fact that, on the historical frontier, homesteaders came into conflict with open-range ranchers who grazed cattle on federally-owned lands; thus, the conflict is between private homesteaders and federally-subsidized ranchers.[41] While this was true in real life, the facts of the matter are virtually never articulated in classical Western films themselves. The role of the American federal government as subsidizer of open range is not addressed in *Shane*, nor is it addressed in *The Man Who Shot Liberty Valance* in which the big land owners employ the homicidal Liberty Valance to enforce their will. Nor is a theme of government collusion with business used in *Jesse James* (1939) in which the railroads are the chief villains, in spite of the fact that the railroads were notorious supporters of corporate welfare on the real-life frontier.

If these films really wanted to point to the state as the source of conflict, why do they virtually never make a government agent a villain? The villains are, almost without exception, businessmen or Indians or the people who collaborate with them. Government agents are usually heroes.

When large business interests do appear as friendly protagonists in film, they are notable for their rarity. Andrew McLaglen's Westerns *McLintock!* (1963) and *Chisum* (1970) present two exceptions to the usual rule, and they assumed that there is "no conflict between the frontier aristocrat and the public welfare."[42] Both *McLintock!* and *Chisum* were later Westerns, however, with Chisum being made well into the period of revisionist Westerns when the structure of the classical Western had almost completely broken down. According to Lenihan, during the 1950s and the high tide of the classical Westerns, only two major Westerns, *The Broken Lance* and *Ten Wanted Men*, employed the same themes as *McLintock!* and Chisum.

---

[41] Ibid.
[42] Lenihan, *Showdown, p. 151.*

In most classical Westerns, when capitalists appear as villains the conflict is generally framed as a simple matter of big business versus small business or small-time farmers. To claim that there is a subtext of free-markets versus government subsidy in classical Westerns is to invent a theme and subplot where none exists. On the contrary, the economics of the Western fit quite well with a primitivist view of modern economies in which advanced economies exploit workers, coerce the public, and rob men and women of their right to live off the land.

This romantic view of subsistence living works to overturn the value placed on industrialization and capitalism as held by the Victorians and the bourgeoisie and ignores the economic realities of modern societies. Murray Rothbard pointed this out in his critique on the division of labor and primitivism. Rothbard contended that not only is modern industrialization necessary to keep the significant bulk of humanity alive, but that modern civilization offers the best hope for a decent standard of living for most of the human race.[43] In the mid twentieth century, the creators of Western films were still heavily influenced by the anti-capitalist stories of the "satanic mills" which, through industrialization, had made ordinary people worse off. In more recent decades, however, economic historians have repeatedly shown that workers' living conditions actually improved due to industrialization, and this became more so as the nineteenth century wore on. Even the communist intellectual and historian E.P. Thompson was forced to concede[44] that the rapidly urbanizing world of the nineteenth century was marked by improvements in the standard of living for a very

---

[43] Murray N. Rothbard. "Freedom, Inequality, Primitivism, and the Division of Labor," in *Egalitarianism as a Revolt Against Nature and Other Essays* (Auburn, AL: Mises Institute, 2000), pp. 247-303.
[44] R. M. Hartwell, *The Industrial Revolution and Economic Growth*, (London: Methuen and Co. Ltd, 1971), p. 373.

large portion of the population "between 1790 and 1840."[45] Had Thompson included the decades following 1840 in his analysis he would have found an even greater increase. These wages were made possible by increases in productivity that resulted from new economies of scale and major industrial development. The industrial revolution made it possible for the bulk of humanity to rise above the most basic levels of subsistence living for the first time. One certainly wouldn't learn this from watching Westerns. Even from its earliest days the Western embraced an unsophisticated view of frontier economics where all men live in a state of virtual equality as they work their lands and trade simple goods for simple necessities at the general store.

The Classical Western and Nostalgic Primitivism

While liberalism developed and enjoyed its greatest influence in an industrializing world where international trade, the division of labor, and the urban landscape became increasingly important fixtures of life, the Western would celebrate primitive modes of living while portraying cities and advanced economic systems as an effeminate corruption of the "natural" human condition.

The Western in its post-dime-novel and cinematic form began in the age of "nostalgic primitivism" where novels and early silent films used the genre of the Western as a means to "redefine the nature of masculine identity in a society increasingly regarded as 'overcivilized' and 'feminized.'" Referring specifically to the early Westerns of Douglas Fairbanks, Gaylyn Studlar identifies the Western in these early years as part of a "widespread effort to redefine American

---

[45] E. P. Thompson, *The Making of the English Working Class* (New York, NY: Pantheon Books, 1963), p. 211.

male identity in response to perceived threats from modernity."[46]

Perhaps the chief popularizer of this revolt against cultured urban life at the close of the nineteenth century was Theodore Roosevelt, a privileged Easterner who had convinced himself that his travels in the American West had somehow made him much more masculine than most of his fellow American men. Roosevelt, like countless others at the turn of the century, believed that camping out in the woods was the best way to achieve "character development" in young boys.[47] According to Studlar, "character-builders embraced a nostalgia for a primitive masculine past. The strongest evidence of the past in contemporary life was the instinct-driven 'savagery' of boys." Ernest Thompson Seton, head of the Boy Scouts of America, would claim that living the primitive life was an "antidote to 'city rot' and the 'degeneracy' of modern life."

In Western after Western, from the earliest days of the genre to even modern times, the hero is set up as an uncultured man of the frontier who is quite contemptuous of the effeminate and urbanized Easterners who cross his path. Over the course of a typical Western tale, the urban fool must learn the ways of the gun or be destroyed. The representative of complex or ineffective Eastern values has little to contribute to the more pure and primitive order established by the tough men of the West.

In John Ford's *Fort Apache* (1948), this theme is immediately clear as Colonel Thursday (Henry Fonda) arrives

---

[46] Gaylyn Studlar, "Wider Horizons: Douglas Fairbanks and Nostalgic Primitivism," in *Back in The Saddle Again: New Essays on The Western*. Eds. Edward Buscombe and Roberta E. Pearson (London: British Film Institute, 1998), p. 63.
[47] Anne Stiles, "Go Rest, Young Man," American Psychological Association, January 2012,
http://www.apa.org/monitor/2012/01/go-rest.aspx

in the Arizona desert quickly declaring that he'd much rather be in Europe than the American West. Thursday simply doesn't understand the ways of the West, and when he refuses to shake hands with a low-ranking cadet, it is apparent that Thursday is far more concerned with the letter of the law practiced in the East than with the more primitive (and presumably better) code of honor that governs the Army on the frontier. Thursday happily works within the restrictions imposed by the civilian government while Kirby York (John Wayne), Thursday's frontier bred number-two, strains under its burden of bureaucracy. At every turn, the Easterners are far less honorable and effective than the frontiersmen who know better. Thursday's ambition and attachment to Eastern ways eventually brings about his downfall as he leads an ill-fated charge against the Apaches.

This theme is repeated in *Rio Grande* (1950) as Kirby Yorke's (he's "York" in *Fort Apache*, but "Yorke" in *Rio Grande*) son must be schooled in the ways of the frontier against the objections of his mother. In *Cheyenne Autumn* (1964), Ford portrays the frontier cavalry as guilty only of following orders when the Eastern bureaucrats hand down orders that lead to the annihilation of the Cheyennes.

In Ford's *The Man Who Shot Liberty Valance* (1962), the film opens with Ransom Stoddard (James Stewart) returning to the small town of Shinbone where he had once been a frontier lawyer. Stoddard is now a successful politician having built his career on his reputation as "the man who shot Liberty Valance." Through a series of flashbacks, the audience learns that Liberty Valance was once an outlaw in Shinbone who terrorized the people of the town and enforced the will of corrupt ranchers who opposed statehood for the territory. Stoddard had initially traveled to Shinbone in order to bring learning, law, and the blessings of civilization to the people of the town. On his way to town, Stoddard himself is attacked by Valance who tears up Stoddard's law books, thus highlighting the irrelevance of book learning on the frontier.

The people of the town, led by an out-gunned marshal, do nothing to protect themselves. Eventually, small-time rancher Tom Doniphon (John Wayne) takes it upon himself to help Stoddard defeat Valance. In a showdown, Stoddard, who is inept with firearms, amazingly kills Valance and becomes a local hero. The death of Valance paves the way for the defeat of the big ranchers and for statehood and the flowering of modern civilization across the territory.

Throughout the film, Stoddard is the symbol of effete Eastern sensibilities that are in tension with the hard-boiled frontier skills of Tom Doniphon and Liberty Valance. Stoddard is concerned with teaching, journalism, the written law, and a variety of other intellectual pursuits that are quickly exposed as useless skills on the frontier. Eventually, Stoddard accepts that order dispensed from the barrel of a gun is what paves the way for law and order, and in one scene, Stoddard poignantly erases a phrase he had written on the blackboard of the town's school: "Education is the basis of law and order."

Although Stoddard had been made out to be a hero by the townsfolk for his killing of Valance, we eventually learn that he had not killed the outlaw at all. It was Doniphon, hiding in the shadows, who shot Valance when Stoddard fired his own gun (and missed) during the showdown with Valance. Doniphon selflessly allows Stoddard to take the credit. Being merely a humble frontiersman, Doniphon believes himself unfit for a leadership role in the rapidly civilizing West.

In all of these cases, the film presents the gunfighter—who in Ford's films is usually a government agent—as the only truly competent defender against threats to the establishment of law and order. Whenever the "simplicity" of the West is victorious over the complexity and corruption of the East, it is due to the Eastern interloper attempting to use law and reason to limited avail while the gunfighter functions much more successfully on blind instinct. Stoddard keeps attempting to reason his way to a solution with Valance, but in the end, this proves useless, as the only thing the men of the West understand is brute force.

Defenders of the Western as exemplar of America's traditional values might claim the Western denigrates industrialized society in order to emphasize the importance of self-reliance and independence. While this may be arguable regarding the myth of the frontier, it nevertheless runs up against the reality of the historical frontier in which self-sufficiency was an unobtainable ideal. As noted by Douglas J. Den Uyl, one can argue "no one in a pre-civilized state can be self-sufficient because the goods needed are simply not available."[48] The gunfighter, ironically, depends on mass-produced firearms for his vocation; and on the real-life frontier, few settlers attempted "self-sufficiency" in a way attributed to the gunfighter. Most everyone depended on trade, contracts, family connections, and church organizations to make a go of it on the frontier. "Self-sufficiency" of the gunfighter type would have had few adherents among the bourgeois classes of nineteenth-century America.

The impetus behind this fondness for savagery and primitivism, as Studlar notes, is a distinct reaction against the urban bourgeois life that characterized the industrialization of the nineteenth century. Richard Etulain attributes some of the popularity of the Western to "the conflict between industrial and agricultural America and the resultant nostalgia for the past." [49] Nostalgic primitivism isn't simply fondness for simpler ways, but an active aversion to the economic system of the contemporary world during the early twentieth century. Referring to the early Westerns of Fairbanks, Studlar writes

---

[48] Douglas Den Uyl, "Civilization and Its Discontents," In *The Philosophy of the Western* (Lexington, KY: University Press of Kentucky, 2010), p. 43.
[49] Quoted in Tompkins, *West of Everything*, p. 27.

In his films, without literally becoming a child, Douglas Fairbanks seemed to achieve a change that many American men in routine-driven, sedentary, bureaucratized jobs yearned for. The onerous psychic and physical demands of masculinity could be held in abeyance by a hero who embodied qualities of intensity, vitality, and instinctual liberation which seemed to many, to be increasingly difficult to acquire and retain among the complacency, compromise, and consumerist comfort of modern bourgeois life.[50]

Criticizing modern bourgeois life and the capitalist system it created then becomes a raison d'être of the Western early on, and the theme of the competent and honest frontiersman against the incompetent and duplicitous Easterner becomes an enduring symbol.

The Gunfighter vs. Bourgeois Life and Ideology

The revolt against the effeminate Easterner in Western film is closely related to the revolt against bourgeois society in general. The Easterner represents a refined, cultured, and literate society at peace. In the worldview of the Western, this sort of society does not produce people suited for self-reliance or sound decision-making on the frontier. While the gunfighter ascends to levels of great virtue and importance in the Western, the institutions of peaceful and private society are regularly mocked and portrayed as corrupting at best, and ridiculous at worst.

While we know that the landscape of the historical West is primarily a landscape of farms, ranches, shops, churches, and homes, the landscape of the cinematic West is a landscape of war inhabited primarily by gunmen and their

---

[50] Studlar, "Wider Horizons," p. 72.

victims. This focus on the frontier society's dependence on the gunfighter pushes all institutions of civilization to the margins and produces a genre that portrays constant violent conflict as a romantic and redemptive activity. Meanwhile, religious devotion, economic pursuits, and domestic concerns are shown to be secondary activities and superfluous luxuries that owe their very existence to the quick draw of the gunfighter.

In the traditional Western, the gunfighter is Nietzschean Übermensch and Hobbesian Leviathan rolled into one. He exists to enlighten others and to impose order on a dangerous world simply by being more proficient at the use of force than his enemies. He is a man apart. He is above the contemptible pursuits of ordinary daily life, and only after he imposes order is peaceful civilization possible. The classical Western thus comes to an important conclusion: without the gunfighter, civilization is impossible.

Reviewing the themes of the classical Western, it becomes apparent that the Western is well situated to buttress claims in favor of an authoritarian garrison state of the nature justified by rhetoric of the Cold War or the War on Terrorism during the mid-twentieth and early twenty-first centuries.[51] In the Western, those who remain preoccupied by economic and domestic interests live rather trite and naïve lives until they embrace the way of the gun. The real conflict is between the non-gunfighters of the frontier, who represent the outdated and dangerous notions of an ill-conceived bourgeois society, and the heroic gunfighter, a symbol of a twentieth-century society much better suited to deal with the harsh realities of the world.

---

[51] Engelhardt, *Victory Culture*, p. 5. Engelhardt examines the role of the Western in Cold War rhetoric as a useful form of propaganda that justifies the exterminations of threats to the American nation state.

Anthony Mann's gunfighters in *The Man from Laramie*, *Winchester '73*, *The Naked Spur*, *Bend of the River*, and *Man of the West* (1958) are all men who emerge from the wilderness and use their skills as former outlaws or wild men to preserve justice. In some cases, they must be always moving, either to avoid danger, or to escape their pasts, or simply to satisfy a need for a transitory life. As a part of the wilderness itself, they emerge to protect the settlers and society in general from the menaces that exist out in the wilds. Their status as uncivilized and wild is what qualifies them to be effective as defenders of the hapless general public in these films, for if they had actually been an ordinary member of civilized society, they would be incapable of defending themselves and others in the aggressive manner required in Westerns.

In Mann's Westerns especially, the hero is virtually incapable of existing in normal society for he is "near-psychotic" as film scholar Paul Willemen describes him.[52] He is motivated by the basest desires such as revenge and greed, but it is this wildness and lack of control that makes him so valuable to the ordinary people in need of his protection.

In Ford's films, the hero is less feral, although just as aloof to being attached to the responsibilities of ordinary society. In all four of his cavalry films, *Cheyenne Autumn* (1964), *She Wore a Yellow Ribbon*, *Fort Apache*, and *Rio Grande*, the hero, always a cavalry officer, has virtually no obligations to any family or property, and his affections are reserved strictly for the Army. Only in Rio Grande does the hero, Kirby Yorke, have living family members at all, and even then he is estranged from them and unfamiliar with the responsibilities of family life.

----

[52] Quoted in Russell West, "This is Man's Country: Masculinity and Australian National Identity in Crocodile Dundee," in *Subverting Masculinity: Hegemonic and Alternative Versions of Masculinity in Contemporary Culture*, ed. Russell West and Frank Lay (Amsterdam: Editions Rodopi B.V., 2000), p.55.

The hero attains his value as an extremely efficient killing machine that is uncomfortable filling roles normally associated with an ordinary middle-class lifestyle. In these films, the hero is more comfortable in the saddle than in a chair and more accustomed to sleeping outside than in a bed. He might be tamed for an evening to engage in the niceties of civilization, such as a bath and a shave, but he must always return to the wilderness where the important action—the heroic action—takes place.

The gunfighter attained his status as protector and indestructible man through his many years away from ordinary civilized people, and he therefore carries with him a natural virtue not possessed by the new arrivals in the West. The primitivist influence on this aspect of the Western is pervasive. Heroism is learned and acted out in the wild, while cowardice and pointless talk take place in the cities and towns and living rooms.

In some cases, the gunfighter's abilities become more enhanced the less civilized he becomes. In Anthony Mann's last Western, *Man of the West*, Link Jones (Gary Cooper) is a family man from the town of Good Hope who is trying to find a teacher for the town's school. Jones finds himself forced into the company of a criminal gang that has kidnapped the innocent female singer Billie Ellis (Julie London). Ellis serves as a symbol of civilization in the film, continually at risk of being raped and killed by the criminal gang. Only Jones stands between the gang and Ellis, and it is eventually revealed that Jones is a former criminal himself, and a murderous and brutal one at that.

In order to protect Ellis from rape, and in order to foil the plans of the criminal gang, Jones must embrace his former criminal self. As he does so, he becomes more cunning and effective as the film's hero. His progression from domesticated family man to criminal illustrates the contrast between the uselessness of cultural refinement in settling the frontier in the face of criminal elements.

Mann used this same device in *Bend of the River* in which protagonist Glyn McLyntock (James Stewart), a former outlaw, wants to become a settled member of the community for which he is serving as a scout for their wagon train to Oregon. When outlaws attempt to steal the wagon train's food, McLyntock finds that he must draw upon all of the skills he learned as an outlaw to defeat the thieves.

This opposition to law-abiding bourgeois behavior that permeates the Western further serves to solidify the values of primitivism in its audience. Link Jones is victimized as he tries to find a schoolteacher for his town, but as he returns to his outlaw instincts he becomes adept at defending himself. At the same time, the seasoned frontiersmen of Fort Apache reject the formalism and refinement of the East, as symbolized by Thursday, thereby saving their comrades. Ransom Stoddard gives up on making education the basis of law and order, turning instead to the gun.

Through the bare-bones efficiency of violent action employed by the gunfighter, instinctual action and frontier justice can be shown to be morally and practically superior to the more civilized notions of systematic thought and the rule of law. Writing on the consequences of primitivism's view of the intellect, Murray Rothbard noted:

> Civilization is precisely the record by which man has used his reason, to discover the natural laws on which his environment rests, and to use these laws to alter his environment so as to suit and advance his needs and desires. Therefore, worship of the primitive is necessarily corollary to, and based upon, an attack on intellect. It is this deep-seated "anti-intellectualism" that leads these people to proclaim that civilization is "opposed to nature" and [that] the primitive tribes are closer to it. . . And because man is supremely the "rational animal," as Aristotle

put it, this worship of the primitive is a profoundly anti-human doctrine.[53]

The gunfighter, not one to rely on deep philosophy or complex argumentation, relies instead on instinct. In *Winchester '73* for example, Lin does not need to deliberate about killing his own brother. He just "knows" that Dutch was born evil (the only explanation provided for his criminal behavior), and is therefore incapable of redemption. Lin cannot realistically attempt to rehabilitate his brother since, in the Western, people are simply good or evil. In classical Westerns, good guys rarely become bad, and bad guys rarely become good no matter how much they may wish to make a change. The conventions of the classical Western require little moral uncertainty or ambiguity, for such things might call into question the absolute righteousness of the final showdown. This extends to relations with Indians. In contrast to earlier Westerns, classical Westerns almost unanimously treat Indians as a uniformly malevolent force.

Essential to this equation as well is the cheapening of the use of language. Talk, which can express more complex and ambiguous ideas than fighting, is viewed with extensive suspicion and is usually the central weapon of the villain against the hero. The most reliable plot device to exhibit this axiom of the genre is the positioning of a slick, charismatic villain against a socially awkward, simply-dressed hero. Hawks uses this device in *El Dorado* (1966) and *Rio Bravo*, but Anthony Mann is particularly proficient at this as shown in *Winchester '73*, *The Man from Laramie*, *The Far Country*, and *Bend of the River* in which the villains talk almost constantly with glib tongues while the hero sits in stony silence. The punch

---

[53] Murray N. Rothbard, "Down with Primitivism: A Thorough Critique of Polanyi," Mises Institute, last modified February 14, 2022, https://mises.org/library/down-primitivism-thorough-critique-polanyi

line of course comes when the antagonist's fondness for talking is revealed as part of his villainy and weakness. Real men, the Western tells us, deal only with actions. Fools and villains, on the other hand, confuse things with talk.

The final lesson to be learned here is that the virtuous Westerner has no need of finely crafted words and slick reasoning to make his way through the frontier. A contract is unnecessary when a handshake will do and a group discussion over a proposed plan of action is foolish when the hero can jump into the saddle and accomplish something. It is always better to be silent and strong. This is the impetus of Nathan Brittles' dubious advice in *She Wore a Yellow Ribbon*: "Never apologize, son. It's a sign of weakness."

The Gunfighter vs. The Victorians

While the Western has little patience for the economic complexities of the market and the industrialized world, it is even more contemptuous of the social and religious life of the Victorian bourgeois world that dominated American culture throughout much of the nineteenth century. The nineteenth-century American middle class, much like the middle class throughout Western Europe, was dominated by bourgeois assumptions about the role of the domestic world in the larger society.

Proper domestic conduct was no small affair. The domestic sphere in the bourgeois world was seen as the fundamental building block of Western civilization. Contemporary defenders of the bourgeoisie from Vienna to San Francisco often contended that it was the family home that made civilization function.[54] Indeed, beyond the factories

---

[54] Susan Isabel Stein, "A Woman's Place: Nineteenth-Century Bourgeois Morality and the Spanish American Domestic Comedy," *Latin American Theatre Review* 26 no. 1 (Fall 1992): pp. 79-90. Victorian domestic values extended even beyond the Victorian

and merchants, the bourgeois home was the symbol of modern liberal society during much of the nineteenth century. The liberal movements during the nineteenth century that attempted (often unsuccessfully) to restrain the nation-state through constitutions and representative governments were, to a large extent, executed with the goal of making the state more accommodating to the property-related pursuits of bourgeois families and individuals.[55]

As the nineteenth century progressed, family and domestic relationships began to change. As the wealth and size of the middle classes throughout America and Europe continued to grow, a considerable number of ordinary families, for the first time in history, could subsist on the income of a single person working outside the home. This was virtually always the husband, so household governance became the central focus of the wives. "Home economics," as we now know it, became very nearly a science during the nineteenth century as middle-class women spent many hours a day in household management and in budgeting the wages earned by their husbands.[56] In many cases, the wife was largely responsible for household management including the physical maintenance of the home, planning for future household needs such as furniture and utilities, and countless other chores considered essential to the economic stability of

---

world. Stein examines several "domestic comedies" produced in Latin America during the nineteenth century which identified "the middle-class household as the locus of decency—the moral core of the social organism." (p. 80.)

[55] The proper governance of private life became a significant concern for cultural leaders of the bourgeois middle class. The role of domestic household management became an important component of larger political and economic concerns as well. See Tracie, Matysik "Sweeping the German Nation: Domesticity and National Identity in Germany, 1870–1945," *Journal of Social History* 43 no. 1 (Fall 2009): pp. 203-205.

[56] Hobsbawm, *Age of Capital*, p. 237.

the family. In Europe especially, even weddings became in many ways a business transaction in which the long-term economic and cultural concerns of families were addressed through economically savvy matchmaking.

Thanks to the surpluses made possible through industrialization, education for women became widespread and homes, educational institutions, and churches became worlds often dominated by women. Women attained more power in the domestic sphere and in churches, where the middle-class women who were fortunate to have discretionary time would devote their resources to a variety of pursuits. Eventually, women would become very active in political movements, whether they were in favor of relieving poverty or abolishing slavery. As the century came to an end, women would be at the forefront of the peace movements against the Spanish-American War and against American entry into the First World War. Women's groups marched against imperialism, slavery, drunkenness, and anything else they saw as a threat to bourgeois domestic life.[57] Not all of these movements were necessarily compatible with the laissez-faire and capitalist sensibilities of many classical liberals of the period, but the centrality of the bourgeoisie to these movement and ideological currents was undeniable.

Today, the Anglo-American version of the bourgeois ideal, Victorianism, is often viewed with disdain, and Victorian imagery is used to conjure up thoughts of sexually-repressed women and psychologically-damaged children living at the mercy of some monstrous patriarch. But those

---

[57] Among these threats to domestic life was "miscegenation" or racial mixing. Douglas in *The Feminization of American Culture* notes the white supremacist overtones present in many Victorian movements in America, although anti-slavery movements and other reformist movements designed to limit the effects of racism in America also simultaneously came out of Victorian society.

who actually lived in the bourgeois world often saw things differently.

Ann Douglas's extensive literary study of this period, *The Feminization of American Culture*, explores the role of women and domestic life in the evolution of religious institutions and literature during the second half of the nineteenth century. Douglas contends that while women remained legally and culturally constrained in their ability to participate in the industrial and political spheres, they asserted themselves through the cultural realm and were able to significantly influence religious and cultural institutions through literature and educational institutions.[58] These female architects of domestic and literary culture "exercised an enormously conservative influence on their society," and that "between 1820 and 1875...American culture seemed bent on establishing a perpetual Mother's Day."[59]

Douglas does not necessarily view this as a positive development. She connects the rise of Victorianism to the rise of consumer and mass culture and concludes that the central problem for the Victorians was consumerism, and that even its culture, which at times relied on both religious and secular sentimentalism, became a type of consumerism itself. According to Douglas, the literature of the age was geared toward mass consumption by readers who were attracted to the middlebrow emotionalism of the Victorian literature of Susan Warner and Harriet Beecher Stowe.

Douglas believes that this sentimental, woman–centered culture sets up the twentieth-century literary revolt against it. Highbrow literature of the second half of the nineteenth century, such as the writings of Herman Melville, was already anti-Victorian, while the middlebrow writings remained bourgeois and middle-class in their outlook. Often attaining bestseller status, these Victorian novels produced dismay

---

[58] Douglas, *Feminization*, p. 317.
[59] *Ibid.*, p. 6.

among some who regarded this literature for the masses as contemptible and prompted Nathaniel Hawthorne to declare "America is now wholly given over to a damned mob of scribbling women..."[60]

Although it dominated book sales during the nineteenth century, Victorian literature was not unchallenged by other fiction. Even before the Western became an influential "literary" form with *The Virginian* in 1902, Victorian literature faced significant competition from the frontier-themed dime novels of the nineteenth century. The dime novels appealed to younger males, and they were bestsellers, especially among the working classes.

It would be a mistake however, to conclude that Victorian novels were for the upper classes, selling relatively few copies, while the dime novels were for mass consumption. Although Douglas herself takes a dim view of mass consumption, the commercial success and popularity of Victorian fiction speaks to its success and influence. Victorian literature was middlebrow, not highbrow, and as such was accessible to a large cross-section of American society. Books like *The Lamplighter* (1854) and *The Wide, Wide World* (1850) were bestsellers, selling hundreds of thousands of copies and spawning countless other books seeking to capitalize on the success of the Victorian literature that came before.

Ann Douglas observes that "Harriet Beecher Stowe wrote the century's biggest best-seller in *Uncle Tom's Cabin* (1852) and consolidated the virtual stranglehold of America's women authors on the fiction market ... White middle-class women had seized the reins of national culture in the mid- and late-Victorian era."[61]

By the time dime novels were being made into silent Western films and Owen Wister and Zane Grey were

---

[60] John T. Frederick, "Hawthorne's 'Scribbling Women,'" *The New England Quarterly* 48, no. 2 (Jun. 1975): p. 231.
[61] Douglas, *Terrible Honesty,* p. 6.

transforming the genre into its modern literary format, Victorian literature was beginning to cede ground to the Western. In her book, *West of Everything*, Tompkins views the Western as an assault on both the bourgeois world of the nineteenth century and on the women who were such an important part of that world. Tompkins' analysis rests on the juxtaposition between the popular literature of the nineteenth century and that of the twentieth. Granted that the Western was the most popular and commercially successful genre of the early twentieth century, Tompkins looks to the Victorian novels that dominated popular fiction through much of the nineteenth. The literature of the nineteenth century, pioneered by female authors like Stowe, Warner, Maria Cummins, and others, could not have been more unlike a traditional Western:

> In these books (and I'm speaking now of books like Warner's *The Wide Wide World*, Stowe's *The Minister's Wooing*, and Cummins's *The Lamplighter*) a woman is always the main character, usually a young orphan girl, with several other main characters being women too. Most of the action takes place in private spaces, at home, indoors, in kitchens, parlors, and upstairs chambers. And most of it concerns the interior struggles of the heroine to live up to an ideal of Christian virtue — usually involving uncomplaining submission to painful and difficult circumstances, learning to quell rebellious instincts, and dedicating her life to the service of God through serving others…there's a great deal of bible reading, praying, hymn singing, and drinking of tea. Emotions other than anger are expressed freely and openly. Often, there are long, drawn-out death scenes in which a saintly woman dies a natural death at home. Culturally and politically, the effect of these novels is to establish women at the center of the world's most important work (saving souls) and

to assert that in the end spiritual power is always superior to worldly might.[62]

Tompkins continues:

> The elements of the typical Western plot arrange themselves in stark opposition to this pattern, not just vaguely and generally, but point for point. First of all, in Westerns (which are generally written by men), the main character is always a full-grown adult male, and almost all of the other characters are men. The action takes place either outdoors —on the prairie, on the main street — or in public places — the saloon, the sheriff's office, the barber shop, the livery stable. The action concerns physical struggles between the hero and a rival or rivals, and culminates in a fight to the death with guns. In the course of these struggles the hero frequently forms a bond with another man — sometimes his rival, more often a comrade — a bond that is more important than any relationship he has with a woman... There is very little expression of emotions. The hero is a man of few words and expresses himself through physical action — usually fighting. And when death occurs it is never at home in bed but always sudden death, usually murder.[63]

The dominance of the Victorian literature would eventually be targeted by what Douglas calls "the moderns" during the early twentieth century. The shift from the Victorians to the moderns in culture would consist, according to Douglas, of a "shift from reform-oriented, serious-minded, middlebrow religious and intellectual discourse to the

---

[62] Tompkins, *West of Everything*, p. 38.
[63] *Ibid.*, p, 38-39.

lighthearted, streetwise, and more or less secular popular and mass arts as America's chosen means of self-expression."[64] In order to complete this change from the sentimental narratives to the more hard-nosed "honest" narratives of the modern world, the moderns needed to overcome "the powerful white middle-class matriarch of the recent Victorian past."[65] The Western, so opposed to the value system of the late Victorians, fits well within this new shift in popular culture.

During the time of the Victorians, however, the themes of Christian virtue and personal endurance of affliction rarely failed to please audiences. To further illustrate this, Tompkins points to Charles Sheldon's 1896 book *In His Steps*, which chronicles the evolution of a congregation as it attempts to live a radically charitable Christian lifestyle. This book was wildly popular. It was translated into 21 languages and sold hundreds of thousands of copies. In this same period, books such as the mega-bestseller *Ben Hur* (1880) and the popular *Quo Vadis* (1895) featured heroes who do not triumph by killing their adversaries but by meekly enduring a series of trials, and ultimately persevering in their faith in God.[66]

Tompkins' conclusion is that the Western, being so hostile to Christianity and to domesticity, is at its most basic level designed to negate the role of women in American society. She undoubtedly has a point here, but she misses the larger point. Her observations on how the Western jettisons most everything dear to middle class Americans during the nineteenth century (i.e., domestic Christian values) take us closer to the truth. The non-essential roles that women play in the Western are certainly emphasized in the films, but the women are not just women in the Western; they are also

---

[64] Quoted in Rob King, *Hokum!: The Early Sound Slapstick Short and Depression-Era Mass Culture* (Oakland, CA: University of California Press, 2017) p. 33.

[65] Douglas, *Terrible Honesty*, p. 7-8.

[66] Tompkins, *West of Everything, p. 30.*

representatives of bourgeois society. As the nostalgic primitivists made clear with their opposition to industrialized society and with their program for achieving manhood in a mud hole, the real loathing being propagated by the Western is not just for women, but for the urban, industrial, bourgeois world that had so radically changed Western civilization. The primitivists may have been (and probably were) misogynists, but their overriding interest was not only in subduing women but also in subduing the larger society they represented.

By mid-century, the Cold War had increased the impetus to devalue the domestic in favor of a global ideological struggle. During the 1950s, popular art like Westerns reminded viewers that few considerations could take precedence over the need to rid the world of communist evil, whether by six-shooter or by intercontinental ballistic missile.

An examination of the Westerns of the very early days of the Western film, however, suggests that Tompkins may be overstating her case regarding early Western silent films. The earliest Westerns of the silent era provide a different take on the genre in numerous ways, from the physical setting to the treatment of Indians.

According to Simmon, the earliest Westerns surprise in several ways:

> When we go back and watch surviving silent Westerns chronologically, there are a pair of subsequent surprises, because of how different the genre looks and because of what different things is has to say in its earliest guises, especially from around 1908-1910. In landscape, Westerns from this era are lush, woodsy, and wet: filled with lakes, streams and canoes, of chases through the underbrush, of hand-to-hand fights through forest clearings. In narrative, many of these Westerns are set entirely within tribal communities or feature a "noble redskin" as guide or savior to the white hero. Only later, around 1911, do we begin to find the

wide vistas, rolling grasslands, arid deserts, and those savage Great Plain Indians wars that now appear so fundamental to the genre.[67]

These trends only last for a few years at a time, but being the earliest days of the genre in film, they set the stage f
or numerous later Westerns.

The early years of the genre were marked by very different sensibilities, particularly in regards to Native Americans. In addition to the "noble redskin" that Simmon mentions, the earliest Western films in many cases made the white settlers out to be villains by comparison. According to Simmon, "White characters…arrive as villainous disruptions to forest idylls, as with the land grabbing pioneers of *The Red Man's View* (1909) or the doctor in *Mohawk's Way* (1910)."

As a brand-new industry, the film industry of this era was composed primarily of small firms located on the East coast. Often, if not usually, Indian characters were played by actual Native Americans. In some cases Native Americans directed the films, as in the case of James Young Deer who for a time was an influential filmmaker in the industry. This practice came to an end as the industry slowly relocated to southern California, but it is an illustration of how much the industry changed between 1910 and 1950.

By the era of the classical Western, Indians had been relegated almost entirely to roles as villains. The somewhat pro-Indian classical Western, *Broken Arrow* (1950), is notable precisely because a Western film sympathetic to the Indians had become such a novelty during the post-war period. During 1910, however, there would have been little novelty to the plot of *Broken Arrow*, which casts the Apache leader Cochise in a positive light.

----

[67] Simmon, *The Invention of the Western Film*, p. 4.

As late as the 1930s, Indians were portrayed much more sympathetically than in the post-war films. In the movie serials *The Miracle Rider* (1935), starring Tom Mix, the protagonist becomes an advocate for the Indian tribes, and early in the series, being told that one group of Indians are traveling cross-country with a large amount of cash, the hero rushes off to protect the Indians from possible highway robbers. He's too late, however, and the Indians fall victim to marauding white men.

In a major departure from the classical Westerns, some early Westerns cast the Indians not only as sympathetic characters, but as examples of virtuous middle-class behavior.

In *The Miracle Rider*, the ambushed and robbed Indians had been carrying savings they had accumulated in order to begin farming operations as part of an effort to settle down and become like the white middle-class settlers.

In the earlier full-length silent film *Hiawatha: The Indian Passion Play* (1913), the Indians welcome Catholic missionaries into their settlement displaying an openness to Christianity exhibited by few gunfighters of the classical Western.

Indians repeatedly exhibit values of hearth and home in contrast to the shiftless white settlers who disrupt established ways of life. In early Westerns based on the works of James Fenimore Cooper, the iconography of the frontier hero is challenged with story lines featuring "talkative Indians and long-winded Natty [Bumppo, the protagonist] himself [who] seem far from Hollywood's taciturn cowboys."[68]

Director D.W. Griffith, certainly a defender of (Anglo-Saxon) bourgeois values in *Birth of a Nation* (1915), brings his own Victorian sensibilities to some early Westerns. Simmon describes Griffith as "the most consistent, and most Victorian, in assigning the highest ethics to women"[69] in his Western films while exhibiting a "lingering Victorian

---

[68] *Ibid.*, p. 14.
[69] *Ibid.*, p. 26.

obsession"[70] with story lines related to the protection of the innocence of children.

This isn't to say that the early Westerns were Victorian narratives taking place in a wilderness setting. The overall elements of nostalgic primitivism are present, as is the gunfighter who metes out justice from a well-aimed rifle. Nevertheless, the early Westerns contradict the core values of nineteenth-century bourgeois literature to a much lesser extent than their mid-twentieth-century descendants.

The hero of the silent Westerns remains a man of the wilds, at least initially, and his intervention is key in paving the way for civilization. He has little use for civilized society in his role as a gunfighter, although he will usually settle down with a woman once the villains have been killed.

Indeed, the centrality of women to the gunfighter is much more prominent in many early Westerns than is the case during the classical period. While revenge, male camaraderie, and noble ideals usually motivate the gunfighter of the classical period, winning over a woman is a major motivator for the gunfighter of the early Westerns. In *The Return of Draw Egan* (1916), the protagonist (William S. Hart), an outlaw who has tricked the residents of a town into making him marshal, decides to go straight permanently and settle down after falling in love with the mayor's daughter, who is "the kind of girl he had heard of but never believed to exist." In *Tumbleweeds* (1925), the hero Don Carver (Tom Mix) is a drifter but his love for a woman motivates the principal action of the film involving an Oklahoma land rush.

The gunfighter's desire for the heroine is central to the plot in these early Westerns. In contrast, while numerous gunfighters of the classical period also eventually settle down with women, the primary motivation of the protagonist stems

---

[70] *Ibid.*, p. 19. At the climax of *Birth of a Nation*, a white Victorian family is under siege by mob of black former slaves, illustrating Griffith's fondness for the Victorian family and white racial purity.

from a desire for money, as in *The Naked Spur*, or revenge, as in *Winchester '73*. The eventual love interest tends to show up late in the film and does not alter the central conflict between protagonist and antagonist. In *Red River*, for example, the love interest (not for protagonist Dunson himself, but for his adopted son) shows up only in the third act, and in *Rio Bravo*, the female lead, Feathers, while a charming character, has no motivational effect on the sheriff's faithful execution of his law-enforcement duties. Just as often, the gunfighter ends up not settling down at all as in *The Man from Laramie*, *Fort Apache*, and *Shane*.

The early Westerns are often much less authoritarian than the Westerns of the classical period as well. The heroes of silent-era Westerns are often outlaws or Indians, and the outlaws are frequently on the run from ineffectual agents of law enforcement. In John Ford's *Stagecoach* (1939), the last of his pre-war Westerns, the *Ringo Kid* is reminiscent of the charming and mostly harmless outlaws played by Tom Mix and William S. Hart during an earlier period. After World War II, Ford departs from this model completely and never again features an outlaw as his protagonist. None of Hawks' heroes from the classical period are outlaws, although Anthony Mann, notable for his more "edgy" Westerns, employs former outlaws as his heroes in *Bend of the River* and *Man of the West*.

Although her critique applies partially to Western films of all periods, Tompkins' critique is most applicable and trenchant when applied to the post-war classical Westerns. With all their sparse landscapes, militarism, masculine focus, and absence of religious faith, the classical Western presents the themes of the Western in their most stark and serious terms. Following the Second World War, the vestiges of Victorianism in the Western are excised almost completely. Women recede even more into the background, while religion, commerce, and domestic concerns become even sparser and of less relevance. Indians become almost uniformly a force for evil, while sheriffs, cavalry and other

59

symbols of government power become even more revered and unchallenged.

The Gunfighter vs. Women

In many Westerns, women serve a function similar to the effete males of the East. They lack an understanding of the ways of the West, and they fail to grasp the monumental importance of the work being performed by the gunfighter. In *Rio Grande*, for instance, Yorke's estranged wife is told by her son that Yorke is a "great soldier," and she responds that "what makes soldiers great is hateful to me." The viewer is not supposed to sympathize with Kathleen when she makes this statement. By the end of the film, she modifies her value system to match his, and Yorke remains unchanged. We are led to conclude that she simply doesn't understand the sacrifices that must be made to bestow the blessings of modern government on the frontier. In *She Wore a Yellow Ribbon*, the hero's wife is long dead, so the hero remains as free to act as *Red River*'s Tom Dunson, who deserts his love interest to build his ranch.

Red River removes any role for women on the frontier through a conversation in the film's opening scene. Dunson explains to his unnamed love interest that he must leave her, declaring that frontier life is "too much for a woman." To this she replies, "You'll need me. You'll need what a woman can give you to do what you have to do." The classical Western, however, makes it clear that a man like Dunson doesn't need a woman at all, and he rides off leaving her with the wagon train. She is killed by Indians several hours later. Dunson then stumbles upon a young orphan in the wilderness. The subsequent adoption of the orphan allows Dunson to acquire an heir without the inconvenience of having a relationship with a woman. It also provides a handy excuse to avoid any themes of domestic life in the film, even though the film is ostensibly about a family dynasty.

Often, women are just obstacles to be overcome. In Fred Zinnemann's *High Noon*, Mrs. Kane allies herself with the cowardly townsfolk and tries to convince Marshal Kane to leave town before the villains arrive. Similarly, in *The Searchers* (1956), after a woman and her older daughter have been raped and murdered by Indians, and a second daughter kidnapped, Ethan Edwards, the hero, is told by an older woman to not encourage the young men to waste their lives in vengeance. Edwards ignores her. He then leads the men on a multi-year, but ultimately successful, revenge-fueled spree across the desert.

In other films, women more explicitly represent civilization. In *My Darling Clementine* (1946), Clementine attempts romantic attachment to Wyatt Earp, yet Earp rejects her so he can ride off to a showdown with the Clantons. He eventually leaves Tombstone altogether (without her) so as not to be compromised by the civilized ways of the growing town. In *The Naked Spur*, protagonist Howard Kemp (James Stewart) is ultimately faced with choosing between the domestic life and the life of an amoral bounty hunter. Lina (Janet Leigh) manages to convince Kemp to settle down with her, but in his surrender to her feminine plan, Kemp's bitterness at leaving the gunfighter's life behind is apparent.

One exception to this trend is Hawks's *The Big Sky* (1952) in which Teal Eye, an Indian woman, is a central character, and assists the two protagonists, Jim Deakins (Kirk Douglas) and Boone Caudill (Dewey Martin), in reaching their destination where they wish to trade with the Blackfeet Indians. Although the film takes place on a frontier, and the villain is a monopolistic fur company, the movie has little in common with the Westerns of the classical period. The fact that one of the main characters decides to stay in Indian country with Teal Eye sets *The Big Sky* apart from most Westerns of this period, as does its setting in the 1830s. Its inclusion of an Indian woman who assists white men is another remnant of the early-silent period that makes its way into a few post-war Westerns. The treatment of Teal Eye could be contrasted with the subplot in The Searchers in which Ethan Edwards' adoptive nephew accidentally buys an Indian wife. The woman is regarded as an impediment to the search party and is treated with general contempt.

Sometimes the women might as well be men. *In The Man from Laramie*, protagonist Will Lockhart is assisted by Kate Canady, a mannish spinster. If women are to be useful on the frontier, it's helpful if, like Canady, they act like men. Canady also presents the film's theory that the villain was made so by a woman. In one conversation, Canady examines the origins of the murderous behavior of Waggoman's spoiled brat of a son, Dave. It is revealed that Dave has turned to a trite and criminal life because his mother, a refined woman of the East, coddled him in his youth.

The choice between a woman and the life of a heroic gunfighter illustrates the fundamental incompatibility that the classical Western assumes exists between bourgeois society and the life of a self-sufficient frontiersman. Although many early Westerns portray the retirement to domestic life as the natural progression of the gunfighter's career, later Westerns of the classical era much more frequently present a gunfighter hero who is a widower or who is generally unresponsive to women. Tom Dunson of *Red River*, Ethan Edwards of *The Searchers*, and Kirby York of *Fort Apache* have little need or use for women. Wyatt Earp refuses to be tied down in *My Darling Clementine*, and Will Lockhart of *The Man from Laramie* rides back into the wild alone. *Shane* of course cannot manage a normal middle-class life.

The Gunfighter vs. Christianity

While women are symbols of domesticity in the Western, they also often represent religion. As *Stagecoach* opens, Dallas, the whore with a heart of gold, is being run out of town by the more conventional and shrewish women who have created a frontier version of the National League of Decency. Dallas' woes are increased by the prejudices of the bourgeois passengers on the stagecoach, with the exception of the charming outlaw, The Ringo Kid. In Mann's *The Far Country*, the women (most of them saloon girls) enthusiastically talk about building churches at some time in the distant future, implying that when churches arrive, the process of settling the frontier will have been complete.

Westerns in general are dotted with occasional references to God, usually made by women, at which point the gunfighter is reliably shown to be made uncomfortable or to shrug off the importance and relevance of religious faith to the conflict at hand.

Christianity in the nineteenth century was not such a marginal and infrequent topic of conversation. As Tompkins and Douglas note above, the popular literature of Victorian America was steeped in Christianity. The popular status of books like *Ben Hur* and *Quo Vadis* illustrates that the Victorian world was a Christian world, and the bourgeois families that lived in it identified themselves as Christian and subscribed to a Christian worldview. Christianity was prominent in their literature, education, and politics. We know that the people who settled the West carried their Christianity with them.[71]

---

[71] According to Louis L'amour in his introduction to the audiobook recording of *A Trail to the West* (Bantam Audio Publishing, 1987), the novels of romantic novelist Sir Walter Scott were particularly popular among frontier settlers, including cowboys and other male laborers. The heroes of Scott's novels were regarded as models for proper behavior on the frontier, L'amour claims, and he suggests that the popularity of Scott's novels were even influential in lowering the incidence of violence against women on the frontier. How Scott was regarded among the Victorians is noted in an 1871 speech by Rev. Charles F. Lee titled "Sir Walter Scott, the Christian Man of Letters" in which Lee claims that Scott's works "describe healthy, manly, Christian characters and in the admiration which they necessarily call forth, they tend to create in the reader a disposition to imitate the virtues which Scott glorifies in them. Having shown that mental greatness

Catholic and Protestant missionaries crisscrossed the frontier, and churches sprang up wherever new towns were founded. In spite of all of this however, the classical Western either ridicules or ignores religion as an important part of the story of the West.

Gunfighters are never religious men. Engaged in the primitive world of the kill-or-be-killed frontier, the gunfighter has no time for such immaterial pursuits. He knows only one thing—physical survival—and no amount of praying is ever going to do him much good. In fact, in some cases, the gunfighter himself serves as a sort of divinity, doling out death and vengeance without the slightest thought that his judgments might be flawed or that he might be gunning down the wrong man. The gunfighter is always right, he always wins the final showdown. He is simultaneously omniscient and omnipotent, and he doesn't need God, for he is a god of sorts—impervious to the dangers and trials that would destroy a lesser man.

This aspect of Westerns is closely related to the anti-intellectualism of the genre, which is not suited to complex philosophical questions. Instead, the Western relies on a moral structure of simplistic dichotomies between good and evil. Later Westerns are notable for their moral ambiguity, but the classical Westerns create a world where the gunfighter destroys the villain with the help of the gunfighter's infallible instincts. When it comes to one's status as a member of the elect or the damned, the characters in Westerns often lack free will since free will would imply an ability to repent of one's evil ways or, conversely, to fall from a state of grace. That fact that characters in Westerns virtually never do either

---

should not be used as a cloak for a bad heart, but, on the contrary, that the possession of great qualities should engender a deeper religious conviction." (Charles F. Lee, "Sir Walter Scott, Christian Man of Letters," *The New York Times*, August 28, 1871.)

illustrates the Western's need to dispense with anything that might complicate the moral landscape.

Since eternal souls don't matter in Westerns, the concepts of the elect and damned retain only a worldly status, but they are nevertheless extremely important in providing justification for the dependence on violence so central to Westerns. Unlike the Victorian novel where saving souls is an important consideration, the Western, through omission, denies the existence of a spiritual world, and exists only in the physical world where elimination of the enemy is the only goal worth considering.[72] Gunfighters occasionally exhibit religiosity, but only in a terse and dismissive fashion. *Red River*'s Tom Dunson mocks Christian Scriptures when on several occasions he guns men down for petty offenses, buries them, and blithely recites the Scripture verse "The Lord giveth and the Lord taketh away," before getting on with the day's chores. In *The Searchers*, Ethan Edwards angrily disrupts a funeral for his dead relatives and then quickly exits the scene. He'd rather be on a horse getting important things done than tending to spiritual trifles. Later, Edwards refers to Christianity as "what you preach" when speaking to Reverend Clayton, putting additional distance between himself and Christianity.

The afterlife is apparently a source of great confusion in Westerns. Following the bloodbath incompetently engineered by Colonel Thursday in *Fort Apache*, York (to the strains of the "Battle Hymn of the Republic") declares that the dead soldiers "aren't forgotten because they haven't died. They're living right out there and they'll keep on living as long as the

---

[72] Redemptive violence is a literary device that dates to the earliest human myths. It states that creative good comes from violence, such as humanity being created from the blood of a murdered god. The term was coined by Christian essayist Walter Wink. (Walter Wink, The Powers that Be: Theology for a New Millennium (New York, NY: Doubleday, 1999).

Army lives." Piles of corpses don't occasion one to mention God—just the Army. In a genre so replete with death, one might think that the characters might consider from time to time a man's ultimate fate, but such thoughts never occur to a gunfighter.

For the gunfighter, what matters is physical survival, and the central concern must be physical life and physical death. The Christian-biblical doctrines that "to die is gain" or that it is better to endure an evil than to commit one, are meaningless in the Western.[73] The Christian ethic is all the more ridiculous since, in the Christian worldview, death may have to be accepted for the sake of defending a larger moral principle. But in the Western, death is defeat, and victory goes to those who live. The Christian God has no value because he is of no use in the classical Western's utilitarian world. The only things that can be trusted in the Western are a ready gun, a steady horse, and a fast draw. The gunfighter may ride for the greater glory of his countrymen and the United States of America, but he most certainly isn't riding for God.

Just as Ford used caricatures of puritanical women as a symbol of religion, Westerns use churches as general symbols of the surrounding bourgeois society. *High Noon* uses this device as a means to exhibit the town's cowardice and hypocrisy. Looking for help against the outlaws, Marshal Kane is determined to gather support from the local church. He interrupts the Sunday service as the minister reads Scripture. While he urgently seeks help, Kane is curtly reminded that he didn't "see fit" to be married in that church: "What could be so important to bring you here now?" Kane simply replies: "I need help." He admits that he isn't "a church-going man," and that he wasn't married there—

---

[73] "To die is gain," from Philippians 1:21, in itself substantially divides the Christian moral ethic from the Western genre's ethic. It is repeatedly reiterated in Westerns that death is the ultimate defeat.

because his wife is a Quaker. "But I came here for help, because there are people here." The cruel and oblivious congregation offers no help.

There are only so many scenes that one can cite here to illustrate the Western's dim view of Christianity because the deafening silence with which the Western treats Christianity and religion so permeates the genre. Neither Mann, Ford, nor Hawks ever see fit to include Christianity as anything other than a minor consideration of those who tend to be an irritant to the hero gunfighter, further illustrating the Western's drastic and lasting departure from the Victorian popular entertainment of the nineteenth century.

In *The Feminization of American Culture*, Douglas points to the influence of the American Victorian women on religious institutions of the period, as well as the perceived shortcomings of their religious culture. Referring to the Victorians, Douglas again employs her view of the Victorians as sentimental and consumerist and contends that "their debased religiosity, their sentimental peddling of Christian belief for its nostalgic value — is crucial in understanding American culture in the nineteenth century."[74]

On this topic, Douglas constructs a theory in which the disestablishment of the churches in America (the end of state-supported religious institutions that came after the American Revolution) led to major changes in American Protestant Christianity during the nineteenth century. Whereas the Christianity of the eighteenth and early nineteenth centuries was more on the hard-line model of Jonathan Edwards, the Christianity of the late nineteenth century took on a much softer, accommodating tone.

The decline of state support for churches led to a need for Protestant clergy to augment financially-supportive church membership by avoiding unpleasant or controversial topics. During this period, Douglas contends, the role of

---

[74] Douglas, *The Feminization of American Culture*, p. 6.

Christian clergy became geared more toward popularization and softening of Gospel themes, and toward supporting women and children in times of emotional need. Ministers switched the focus toward playing a supportive role instead of a demanding and morally absolutist leadership role, as had been the case in earlier centuries. Doctrinal rigor took a back seat to filling the pews with paying believers. Many saw this as a positive development, and Douglas recounts a "vision" related by one Unitarian minister who imagined that the Christian church had transformed itself from an eagle, a symbol of the older faith, into a dove that ministered to children. Although the Unitarian minister meant this to be received positively, this trend within American Christianity, some complained, had produced a "largely pacifist" clergy that "hovered on the edge of the battlefield."[75] According to critics, this was true of both literal wartime battlefields and of moral and philosophical battlefields.

As a result, critics increasingly saw the American clergy as effeminate and intellectually immature. By the early twentieth century, as bourgeois liberalism gave way to progressivism among Victorians, this version of the faith gave birth to what is now known as the "social gospel" of left-wing Victorian reformists.

The movements spawned by the social gospel were more post-Victorian than Victorian, peaking in the early twentieth century. Closely associated with the Progressive movement, the adherents of the social gospel were largely anti-capitalist which puts them at odds with the bourgeois liberal Victorians of 50 years earlier. It is easy to see, however, how the social gospel and the supremely mild version of Christianity described by Douglas could be thought of as synonymous with the Victorians and bourgeois liberals of the nineteenth century.

---

[75] *Ibid.* p. 20

This new mild and pleasant gospel, now associated with the late Victorians, would lead to a backlash. Reflecting on these new strains of Christianity, Richard Niebuhr eventually pronounced his judgment on what he saw as the deterioration of American Christianity during this period, declaring that Americans had embraced a gospel in which "a God without wrath brought men without sin into a kingdom without judgment through the ministrations of a Christ without a cross."

According to Douglas, the moderns of the twentieth century dispensed with what they saw as this contemptuous religious tradition. The moderns introduced very different religious sensibilities in twentieth century literature in general, represented across the spectrum from Hemingway to Fitzgerald to Mencken.

In a similar way, the Westerns' response to Niebuhr's complaint was not to embrace a more doctrinal or hard-line version of the faith, but to replace Christianity's deity altogether. What could be a better answer to the feminized Victorian God than the gunfighter himself? With no true God of any consequence to exact vengeance, the classical Western's gunfighter himself would supply wrath and judgment while bearing a cross of solitude to rid the world of sin.[76]

One of the most well-developed examples of the burden carried by the gunfighter is found in John Ford's *The Searchers*, which emphasizes the gunfighter's separation from domestic and bourgeois society. Edwards is an extreme version of other post-war heroes in John Ford's Westerns. Ethan is not only a Confederate, which makes him rare among Ford protagonists, but he also has a sketchy past in general, as emphasized by an unexplained three-year absence. Almost all

---

[76] In the Pilot of *Hell on Wheels*, the protagonist Cullen Bohannon is asked if he believes in "a higher power." His response: "Yes sir, I wear it on my hip."

of Ford's post-war heroes are former or current lawmen, or are military men. Edwards, on the other hand, was on the wrong side of the Civil War, which perhaps made it easier for the nationalistic Ford to make Edwards a character filled with such a thirst for vengeance.

Film critics and modern fans have made much of Edwards' hatred of Indians, especially Comanches. This hatred drives him to nearly murder his own niece, Debbie, who had become one of the wives of the Comanche Chief Scar. Many now assume that Ford was making an impassioned argument against racism with *The Searchers*, but that is not clear. Edwards' hatred is not based on some arcane and pseudo-scientific theory of race such as those employed by many white supremacists. Nor is his hatred directed toward all Indians. Ethan's hatred of some Indians is based on very concrete experiences in which Indians have raped and murdered his family members. He's motivated more by revenge than by a theoretical idea of race. The Indians are in no way misunderstood innocents in *The Searchers*, and while we learn that Scar is also motivated by a similar thirst to avenge the deaths of his children at the hands of white men, the film's focus is nevertheless on the violence committed by Indians. Ethan's hatred is therefore understandable and arguably justified in the moral context of the film. Ethan only steps over a line (according to the film's moral code) when he tries to kill his niece. Thanks to the intervention of Debbie's adopted brother Martin, she is spared. Later, Ethan repents of his hatred for Debbie, and after scalping Scar, who was killed by Martin, Ethan takes Debbie, who does not resist, home to her white family.

Although Edwards' character is seen by many today as a commentary on racial hatred, he is more properly seen as well within the tradition of the flawed gunfighter heroes. In fact, his character is reminiscent of Anthony Mann's revenge-driven characters, such as Lin in *Winchester '73* who guns down his own brother. In spite of his animalistic hatred, Lin remains the hero.

Unlike Lin, however, Ethan Edwards remains isolated from the community in the model of Shane or Wyatt Earp in *My Darling Clementine*. This is famously emphasized in the final scene of The Searchers in which the door of the family cabin is shut on Edwards who remains outside and alone. What comes immediately before the closing of the door, however, is important also: the scene in which Debbie is brought home to her family for a joyous, if bittersweet, reunion.

Obviously, Ethan Edwards is the man who made this happen. It was his obsession, drive, and frontier know-how that led to the family's reunification and the death of the vicious Comanche Scar. Although she had initially resisted being returned to her white family, Debbie is clearly not resistant to the idea by the end of the film. Edwards' hatred of Indians was not enough to blot out his role as the man who saved a young woman and rid the frontier, with the help of official law enforcement officers, of at least one band of rapists and murderers.

Ethan's ultimate isolation as nature's instrument of vengeance and justice are dramatized in several ways, including his explicit rejection of religious matters, in the person of Reverend Clayton, and everyone else, including their conventional ideas of morality. Emphasizing his status as a man apart and as one who is only hindered by the ordinary people of the frontier, Edwards declares: "Well, Reverend, that tears it! From now on, you stay out of this. All of ya. I don't want you with me. I don't need you for what I got to do."

The Gunfighter vs. The People

Few Westerns offer as stark a portrayal of the classical Western's dim view of American bourgeois society as Ford's *Two Rode Together* (1961). In it we see the development of many of the anti-bourgeois themes that permeate his films. The film is laden with stereotypical portrayals of gullible

Eastern settlers, cynical businessmen, and spiteful, gossiping women.

The film opens with Army officer Jim Gary (Richard Widmark) recruiting Guthrie McCabe (James Stewart) to help him track down abducted whites living among the Indians. McCabe is a corrupt and jaded lawman, but he agrees to the job after he secures some attractive benefits for himself. At the settlers' camp, McCabe is accosted by numerous parents still looking for their children who had been abducted by the Comanches years earlier. The chance of finding the children (now adults) and determining which ones belong to which parent is extremely low. The parents are desperate and pathetic. Sheriff McCabe, on the other hand, shines as a paragon of manly virtue and courage next to the self-important businessman, Mr. Harry J. Wringle, who cynically explains that all he needs is any white male he can pass off to his wife as their son.

Eventually, McCabe manages to bring back two captives from the Comanche camp: one white male and one Mexican woman. The white male, a teenage boy, now thinks of himself as a Comanche and no longer speaks English. McCabe encourages compassion for the young man, but the settlers can't be bothered to do much other than lock him up. The bigotry of the settlers prevents them from seeing him as one of their own, and the settlers treat him more poorly than he was ever treated by the Comanches. The young man turns out to be the brother of one of the female settlers, but before his sister can figure this out, he kills one of his captors and is lynched by a vicious mob of settlers. Later, the women of the settlement ostracize the Mexican woman Elena, the other former captive, for being an Indian's concubine. The settler women believe that Elena should have killed herself rather than submit to such an unseemly fate. In the end, McCabe lectures the townspeople on their lack of tolerance, and he rides out of the settlement with Elena.

So ends another Western, with naïve, selfish, and hypocritical townsfolk being shown the virtuous path by the sheriff, the military man, or some other gunfighter who can rise above the insipid prejudices and dysfunctional bourgeois ways of the people he is selflessly serving. *Two Rode Together* is one of Ford's last Westerns and, like *The Man Who Shot Liberty Valance* and *Cheyenne Autumn*, *Two Rode Together* is a more melancholy and pessimistic film than his earlier efforts. Yet the anti-bourgeois attitude is very much in line with the Westerns of the 1950s. The settler-gunfighter dynamic in *Two Rode Together* is extremely similar to that found in *The Tin Star* (1957) and *High Noon* (1952) where the gunfighter educates the settlers on how to abide by their own professed values. *Two Rode Together* manages to posit a scathing critique of Eastern bourgeois society while setting the gunfighter in a position of moral ascendancy. In his primitive state he is nonetheless more civilized than the hypocrites who claim to be civilizing the frontier.

The relationship between the gunfighter and the townspeople in Stevens' *Shane* is more subtle. In this case, the gunfighter is merely contrasted with the people rather than pitted against them. Although the townspeople would ideally like to rid themselves of Ryker, the local oppressive cattle baron, the townspeople lack the knowledge, courage, and drive to do so. Farmer Joe Starrett does have the courage, but only because he doesn't understand the magnitude of the threat presented by Ryker's gunmen. When Starrett tries to defend the town himself, Shane beats him up and incapacitates him, presumably for his own good, so that Shane can dispense justice himself. Shane here exemplifies the wandering gunfighter archetype and serves as a sort of deus ex machina of the frontier who makes civilization possible. Shane explicitly states he is a relic of an earlier age, but in the end, civilization is not possible without the rootless wanderer who intervenes unasked and makes the town safe for civilization.

The ending of *Shane* harks back to Ford's *My Darling Clementine*. While Wyatt Earp leaves Tombstone voluntarily, however, Shane leaves the town because he simply doesn't fit in there and cannot stay. He can't settle anywhere. He must travel from place to place, perhaps making civilization possible for other towns. He has nothing in common with the townsfolk who owe him everything, but who for the most part don't realize it and likely are not properly appreciative of Shane's role.

The wagon train sub-genre of the Western often features similar relationships between gunfighter and settler. In Anthony Mann's *Bend of the River* (1952), Glyn McLyntock has been hired by the wagon train members to act as trail guide from Missouri to Oregon. McLyntock, however, carefully hides a scar on his neck from a time he was nearly hanged during his days as an outlaw in Bleeding Kansas.[77] He hopes to be accepted as a member of the community some day, but knows that if his past is discovered, he will be expelled from the community. Although the audience can plainly see that McLyntock is on the level, the people of the wagon train are not as perceptive, and the prejudice and intolerance for "bad apples," as the film puts it, is a major plot device in the film. The villain of the film, Emerson Cole, who is very similar to McLyntock, nevertheless decides to return to a life of crime precisely because he despairs of being accepted into an ordinary community like that of the wagon train. McLyntock remains hopeful, however. Even after many trials in which he repeatedly proves his loyalty to the wagon train, Jeremy, the leader of the wagon train, still doubts that McLyntock can really be trusted to be one of them. Only after McLyntock finally kills Cole does Jeremy decide that McLyntock isn't a bad apple after all.

In Henry Hathaway's *True Grit* (1969), the semi-comedic tone of the film did not, according to Lenihan,

---

[77] "Bleeding Kansas" was the name given to a period of civil unrest, lawlessness and guerilla warfare in the Kansas Territory just prior to the U.S. Civil War.

negate the sincerity of the contrast between this honorable rugged individual and an unappreciative, settled society. Instead of thanking [protagonist] Cogburn [played by John Wayne] for capturing notorious outlaws, the town court righteously questions his being too quick to kill his quarry rather than bringing them to trial. The same society that condemns Cogburn's violent ways is seen early in the film turning a public hanging into a festive celebration.[78]

Here we find themes similar to those developed in *Two Rode Together*. Namely, judgmental, incompetent settlers fail to understand the more virtuous way of the gun, yet still manage to find macabre and hypocritical joy in hangings.

In *Bend of the River* and *True Grit*, the hero, who is clearly trying to save the lives of the members of the wagon train or settlement, is nevertheless regarded with suspicion, and even sometimes derision, until he finally proves himself through a wide variety of harrowing trials. The reluctance of the people to accept a clearly virtuous outsider into their community illustrates their lack of generosity and openness to the gunfighter whose skills have made the safety of the community possible.

Sometimes the gun-slinging outsider saves the unreceptive townsfolk from oppressors by pursuing a personal vendetta. In *The Man from Laramie*, protagonist Will Lockhart (James Stewart) frees an entire town from an overbearing cattle baron and his criminal son. While this is ultimately a public service, Lockhart's is motivated by a selfish desire to find the man who is selling rifles to the Apaches.

---

[78] Lenihan, *Showdown*, p. 153.

The film begins with Lockhart entering the vicinity of the dusty town of Coronado. We find out quickly that he is investigating the sale of repeating rifles to the Apaches and that this is a personal matter for him since his younger brother, a member of the U.S. Cavalry, was killed in a recent Apache raid on a Cavalry detachment.

Lockhart soon runs afoul of Dave Waggoman, the irresponsible son of local cattle baron Alec Waggoman. The father and son, and most everyone else Lockhart encounters in town, repeatedly attempt to get him to leave town permanently. It is a "one-man" town, he is informed, and everything "within a three-days' ride" belongs to Waggoman. As the mystery unfolds, Lockhart learns that Dave Waggoman and Waggoman's ranch foreman Vic Hansbro are indeed selling repeating rifles to the Apaches.

According to the film, this is insidious on several levels. Not only did the sale of such rifles make the killing of Lockhart's brother possible, but Lockhart makes it clear that continued sales of rifles to Apaches will make a general Indian uprising possible, leading to the destruction of Coronado and the surrounding white settlements.

When confronted with the fact that women and children would die in such an uprising, Dave Waggoman, being a capitalist motivated primarily by greed, declares, "they aren't mine." Although he is unaware of the sale of the guns, the film implicates Alex Waggoman as a collaborator with the Indians. As an illustration of Waggoman's concern with petty matters of business rather than the more important business of subjugating the Indians, the film reveals that Waggoman allows the Indians to hunt on his land as part of "the deal." Waggoman even challenges the film's assumed innocence of the U.S. Cavalry by declaring that in the battle between Lockhart's brother's unit and the Apaches, "I don't know who shot first, do you?" Lockhart does of course know who shot first, telling Waggoman, "I know the U.S. Cavalry."

Lockhart, unlike Waggoman, and unlike the people of the town, is not motivated by the bourgeois concerns of money and land. He states, "I've never owned any land, and I've never wanted to." The audience eventually finds out that Lockhart is in fact a former cavalry officer and not just a mere private citizen. As a military man, he is motivated by higher ideals.

As he gets closer to solving the mystery, an Indian who works for Waggoman as a clerk at the mercantile frames Lockhart for murder, and Lockhart is locked up by the useless sheriff who clearly does little more than the Waggomans' bidding. Kate Canady, a small-time rancher who is the only person in town who offers Lockhart any concrete help, eventually bails out Lockhart. Even Canady, however, admits she is primarily motivated by her desire to cripple her competition, Waggoman's ranch.

After Lockhart's meddling begins to endanger the transfer of rifles to the Indians, Vic Hansbro kills Dave Waggoman in self-defense after Waggoman begins wildly threatening to kill Hansbro and almost everyone else he knows. Later, Hansbro accidentally forces the elder Waggoman over a cliff in an effort to cover up Dave Waggoman's killing and the sale of the rifles.

At the climax, Lockhart gets the drop on Hansbro and forces him to push the wagon of repeating rifles off of a cliff. Lockhart then runs Hansbro off unarmed, and Hansbro is subject to the typical fate reserved for men who dare do business with the enemy: He is killed by the same treacherous Indians whom he had attempted to furnish with weapons.

Although they remain blissfully unaware of the truth, and had tried to rid themselves of him, the people of the town of Coronado owe Lockhart much. Lockhart, after all, spared the town the misrule of petty tyrant Dave Waggoman. He also spared them death at the hands of the Indians who would have been armed by parochial-minded capitalists looking out only for themselves.

While gunfighters often face foolish, clannish and judgmental settlers and townsfolk, we must consider two exceptions to this model among classical Westerns: John

Ford's *Wagon Master* (1950) and *The Magnificent Seven* (1960), directed by John Sturges.

The Magnificent Seven features freelance gunmen who intervene for the sake of a village, but in this case, their assistance is solicited and financed by the villagers themselves. The film offers a contrast to many Westerns featuring lone sheriffs or gunfighters resisting an invading group of villains. The contrast is found in the fact that the villagers are actively seeking the assistance of the gunfighters and are in charge of the situation. The villagers are in a business relationship with the gunfighters and are their employers, albeit there is an element of selflessness on the part of the gunfighters who are working for low pay. It is the villagers who initiate and take action to protect themselves from a ruthless band of outlaws. At the climax, the villagers even join forces with the gunfighters, attacking their criminal oppressors with chairs, axes and clubs. This sort of mob violence against villains in classical Westerns is noticeably rare, and reasonably so, since the heroism of the gunfighter can more easily be accentuated when compared to a village full of cowards.

In *Wagon Master*, the wagon train, composed of Mormons who must deal with the prejudices of the non-Mormons throughout the frontier, hire two horsemen as guides and security. The two men eventually prove invaluable in protecting the wagon train people from attacks by a murderously criminal gang composed of members of the Clegg family.

Wagon Master is unlike any other post-war Ford Western. It is relatively non-violent, features peaceful interactions between white men and Indians, and focuses more on the wagon train's physical obstacles in the frontier than with the problem of criminal elements. There is more than one dance sequence, and the soundtrack is composed largely of optimistic folk songs sung by the Sons of the Pioneers. The hired gunmen in the film are portrayed more as laborers than professional gunfighters, and the wagon train members themselves are portrayed as being polite, accepting, and generally savvy.

In other words, *Wagon Master* departs from the classical Western in a number of ways. In its lack of violence and its emphasis on family and community life, it resembles Ford's pre-war silent films. Indeed, numerous critics note that the film in both style and content is in many ways a throwback to Ford's pre-war style. The fact that *Wagon Master* is so different from the classical Westerns of the post-war period helps illustrate the changes that took place from the relatively optimistic and family-oriented silent Westerns of the 1920s to the more violent and bleak Westerns of the 1940s and 50s.

Wagon Master and *The Magnificent Seven* are both unusual for the post-war period in their portrayals of civilian and community life as competent and courageous, and as being at least as important as gunfighters in the preservation and settling of the frontier. They stand out from a crowded field of classical westerns in which settlers are craven, ungrateful, and incapable of self-defense. Whether it's the parochial and greedy settlers of *Two Rode Together* or the selfish townsfolk of *High Noon*, the common folk of the classical Westerns are rarely deserving of the magnanimous services provided by sheriffs and cavalrymen and lone gunfighters, yet it is these cowards and fools of the villages and towns who are presumably the progenitors of modern American society in the West.

The Transformation of the Western

By the mid-1960s the Western had changed. The old view of the settlement of the frontier as triumphant progress in the face of savagery had broken down. While the Western was never static as a genre, big-budget Westerns of the 1940s and 50s had generally followed reliable formulas that we now easily recognize as part of the tradition of classical Westerns.

Part of the reason for the change was the fact that the directors dominating Westerns for two decades were reaching the end of their careers. In 1964, John Ford released his last Western, *Cheyenne Autumn*. Howard Hawks continued to make Westerns until 1971, although both Westerns produced after 1959's *Rio Bravo* followed identical traditional Western plot formulas. Anthony Mann directed no Westerns after 1958.

Every scholar of the Western has a theory about the genre's evolution from its classical form to the darker and more ambivalent revisionist form. The Westerns of the post-classical age would prove to be more pessimistic, more graphic in portrayals of violence, and far less likely to portray the frontier as a place of rejuvenation. A common explanation for this change is that the Vietnam War and the crisis of legitimacy that the United States suffered during the 1960s and 70s fueled a breakdown in the traditional mythology of the West. Perhaps it was the assassination of Kennedy, the Age of Aquarius, or Watergate, but one thing was clear: the image of the American gunfighter as harbinger of civilization in a wild land no longer had the same moral authority it once held.

It had been six decades since the first full-length Western novel, *The Virginian*, had redefined the Western as serious adult fiction apart from the dime novels of the nineteenth century and spawned a new era for the genre. Regardless of the cause for its decline, the classic Western no longer seemed to have much to say that the American audience wished to hear. Consequently, the new directors who came on the scene began to rework the Western in new and inventive ways. By 1965, Sergio Leone and Sam Peckinpah had created new Westerns with much different visions that lacked the triumphant militarism of the traditional Westerns.

The Rise and Decline of the State in the Western

When comparing the classic Westerns with the late Westerns, what becomes most immediately obvious is the decline in the prestige of government institutions. The fact that late Westerns have a largely negative view of the nation-state is not in dispute, although the causes for this are debated. To see this, we need not look much further than the portrayal of gunfighters as lawmen in Westerns.

In the classical Western, the gunfighter is most frequently a government agent of some kind. Cavalry officers, federal marshals, and local sheriffs were all popular gunfighter heroes. As noted above, almost all of John Ford's post-war Westerns feature government agents as the protagonists. There are only three exceptions: *Wagon Master*, *The Man Who Shot Liberty Valance*, and *The Searchers*. *Wagon Master* and *Liberty Valance* approach the American nation-state explicitly as the inevitable result of progress, although the state itself is largely absent from the screen. In *The Searchers*, however, government agents play an important support role in the elimination of the Comanche Scar.

This cooperation is particularly interesting in light of Ford's treatment of former Confederates throughout his films. Ford's nationalism comes through in his repeated return to the theme of reunification between North and South. In his cavalry Westerns, it is common to find a scene in which a Confederate veteran who has joined the U.S. Cavalry following the war is killed by Indians. The other soldiers, all Northerners, gather around to commemorate the Confederate's passing as the soundtrack plays a few bars of Dixie. The point of course is to show the valor in Southerners fighting for the Union and to illustrate the rise of American unity since the war, with Northerner joining Southerner in the fight against the savages on the frontier.

Anthony Mann employs a similar device in *Winchester '73* when Lin helps a group of Union cavalry soldiers fend off a band of Indians. The commanding officer declares "I wish I had you with me at Bull Run." Lin responds that he had been at Bull Run, but on the Confederate side. The two former enemies shake hands and bond over a pile of nearby Indian corpses. In *Ambush at Cimarron Pass* (1958), which included an early starring role for Clint Eastwood, embittered former

Confederates reconcile with Union soldiers on the post-war frontier in order to confront the hostile Indians. Former divisions within the nation-state itself are put aside in the classical Western so that a common enemy, the Indians, may be defeated.

In addition to delivering messages about national unity, the classical Western often goes to great pains to ensure that the violence employed by the gunfighter is sanctioned by the community at large. An often-seen exchange in classical Westerns is a scene in which the good guys are all deputized by the sheriff or the marshal right before the final showdown. This change in legal status for all the heroes involved naturally supplies legitimacy and legal immunity to the gunfighters as they prepare to gun down their enemies. Howard Hawks's *Rio Bravo* and *El Dorado* are particularly notable for the careful attention they pay to the issue of legitimate and illegitimate power. In both films, the sheriff collects a band of scrappy allies to defend the town against the villainous ranchers and outlaws beyond the edge of town. The close-knit band of deputies combs the town for outlaws and enjoys the support of various townsfolk in the process. When it comes to the showdown, however, the sheriff and his deputies are isolated by their elevated status as professional lawmen, and they must protect themselves until additional official law enforcement personnel can arrive from far off federal installations. This power of legitimacy is conferred on select men by the sheriff himself, who, we are shown, also confers the approval of the entire community.

Sheriff John Chance (John Wayne), whose benevolent rule maintains peace in the cow town of *Rio Bravo*, Texas, dominates the storyline of *Rio Bravo* (1959). Chance arrests a man for murdering an unarmed bystander in a saloon. The arrested man turns out to be Joe Burdette, the brother of wealthy rancher Nathan Burdette. Following his brother's arrest, the powerful Burdette lays siege to the town in order to prevent Chance from handing over Joe for trial. Realizing that he needs help to defend the town from Burdette and his men, Chance sets to work organizing a posse and enlisting help from townspeople.

Rio Bravo is often described as a response to *High Noon* in which the townspeople refused to help the marshal defend the town. *Rio Bravo* presents a scenario in which the townspeople are generally helpful, although the film is no less authoritarian. It is Chance's force of character and his status as sheriff that makes the defense of the town possible. Learning that Chance is attempting to put together a defense force, the benevolent merchant Wheeler starts spreading the news that Chance seeks assistance. Chance tries to put a stop to this, however, noting that the wrong elements might use this information to their advantage. This is the frontier version of loose lips sinking ships, and the audience learns that Chance's efforts are best protected by maintenance of state secrecy.

Chance deputizes a rag-tag group composed of sidekick Stumpy, recovering drunk Dude, and a young gunslinger, Colorado. Chance makes Dude's contribution possible by helping him overcome his alcoholism. Chance also attempts to deputize Colorado who initially refuses to help, claiming that "minding my own business" is what he's better at than gunfighting. After Burdette's men murder his employer, Colorado attempts to join Chance's group but is angrily turned away by Chance for Colorado's earlier lack of civic-mindedness. Only after Colorado helps Chance kill some of Burdette's men is he finally allowed to come to the town's defense. Chance and his group finally neutralize Burdette and his private gang, and this allows the federal government to arrive and take Joe Burdette away to stand trial.

Meanwhile, there appears to be no civilian government of any consequence in *Rio Bravo*. Chance has total authority to make unilateral choices at will. The enemy, predictably, is a rancher using his wealth to unleash murderous cowhands upon the town. Chance's unimpeachable conduct and the behavior of several townspeople who are not only helpful, but also know their place in relation to Chance, turn *High*

Noon on its head without challenging the position of the lawman at the top of the town's hierarchy.

Hawks made two more films very similar in plot and structure to *Rio Bravo*, with *El Dorado* (1967) and *Rio Lobo* (1971). Even in the second half of the 60s and during the early 70s when Peckinpah and Leone were already challenging the conventions of the classical Western, Hawks was sticking to the tried and true classical formula. *Rio Lobo* and *El Dorado* relied on the same overall messages of law and authority, and John Lenihan notes that *Rio Bravo* and the two remakes assume a frontier where "law and order depends upon professionalism in wielding a gun. The hero of Hawks's films stands with his professional colleagues between order and chaos, with little direct reliance upon the larger society."[79]

Gunfighters might also receive legitimacy through public acclamation. In *The Far Country* (1954), it is significant that when the public demands that Jeff Webster (James Stewart) confront the corrupt sheriff from the neighboring town (he's allied with some villainous business interests), it is not suggested that Webster confront the sheriff as a private citizen. First, he must accept public election as the town's legitimate law enforcement chief. Only then may he pursue a showdown. The film uses this as an opportunity to compare private, selfish interests (such as tending to one's private property), with serving the common good as a government agent. At first, Webster is inclined to mind his own business and work his claim. The moral repugnance of such a self-interested position is belabored repeatedly in the film until Jeff finally recants and accepts responsibility as a public servant, sending the message that bad things happen because good men aren't willing to run for public office.

While public acclamation is good when the sheriff-to-be is a good guy, it's necessary to keep a tight lid on power when undesirables might end up in power. In Mann's *The Tin Star*

---

[79] Lenihan, *Showdown*, p. 153.

(1957), Anthony Perkins plays Ben Owens, an inexperienced sheriff who takes charge only after his father, the previous sheriff, has been killed in the line of duty. The town agitator, Bart Bogardus, who is quite convinced that he could do a better job as sheriff, torments the sheriff from time to time. Fortunately for Owens, Morg Hickman (Henry Fonda) rides into town, reveals that he is a former sheriff himself, and agrees to teach Owens how to deal with agitators like Bogardus. Owens learns from Hickman that "if the Sheriff doesn't crack down on the first man who disobeys him, his posse turns into a mob."

Mob rule is a big problem for Owens since Bogardus is always inciting the townspeople to rebel. Much of this stems from Bogardus's militant racism, which is exposed when he refuses to be disarmed after shooting a half-breed Indian: "No sheriff's gonna disarm no white man for shootin' a mangy Indian. What are ya, an Injun lover?" The townspeople in *The Tin Star* are putty in the hands of whoever is most adept at bullying them. So Owens learns to bully them. If Bogardus, the racist small businessman, is allowed to retain control of the mob, then chaos will reign; but if the sheriff takes charge and "cracks down" on those who disobey him, order will be restored. The sheriff eventually has to face down his own town as they attempt to lynch his prisoners. Bogardus is reined in, mob justice is avoided, and goodness prevails.

Lenihan has pointed out that *The Tin Star* draws heavily on *High Noon*, which also features a sheriff who must confront the ignorant and cowardly people of his own town. *The Tin Star* however, goes a step further in saying that the best frontier towns are those where the sheriff keeps the citizenry on the straight and narrow with a fast draw and a big shotgun. Outlaws aren't the problem. It's the entire population that's the problem, and only a police state will keep the mob in line.

Such depictions of a benevolent order secured by the quick draw of the gunfighter would grow increasingly rare as the 1960s progressed. As with Morg Hickman in *The Tin Star*, the gunfighter of the traditional Western eventually provides his services with benevolence and compassion. They might show reluctance at first, but in the end they always chose to defend the community in need, sometimes even at potentially great cost to self.

The Westerns of Peckinpah, Leone, and Eastwood, on the other hand, feature gunfighters who held no such feelings of good will. Leone's stock character, The Man with No Name, played by Eastwood in three of Leone's films, is a thoroughly self-interested loner who only for very brief moments expresses much interest in anything other than private profit. Peckinpah's protagonists can be actively menacing.

Peckinpah's *Major Dundee* (1965), for example, is a cavalry film where the cavalry is led by a nearly-mad Union commander. The commander, Amos Dundee (Charlton Heston), commonly abuses his own men, invades Mexico against orders, picks a fight with the occupying French forces, and partakes in not one, but two bloodbaths as the film draws to a close. In *Pat Garrett and Billy the Kid* (1973), Pat (James Coburn), newly appointed sheriff, betrays his old friend Billy (Kris Kristofferson) and guns him down as a service to the New Mexico territorial government, which is controlled by a corporate-crony regime. In both cases, the cavalryman and the sheriff, traditionally heroic characters in Westerns, are suddenly murderous villains sowing discord wherever they go.

Sergio Leone's Westerns seldom feature any government agents as prominent characters. In general, such agents in Leone's Westerns are either irrelevant or corrupt as in *Once Upon a Time in the West* (1968) and *The Good, the Bad, and the Ugly* (1966). Union soldiers in *The Good, The Bad, and the Ugly* are particularly monstrous, and the federal soldiers prove to be the most snarling, violent, and corrupt people on the frontier. The one Union soldier with a conscience can only manage to face the absurdity of it all by maintaining a perpetual state of drunkenness. This is all part of the film's profoundly critical view of the nation-state in wartime. Taking place against the backdrop of the New Mexico theatre of the American Civil War, the film portrays the war as a pointless sideshow to the much more interesting and reasonable business of finding buried gold on the frontier. The greed of the protagonists appears quite sane, and even charming, against the senseless carnage of the war that surrounds them. "Blondie" (Clint Eastwood) even offers a puff on his cigar to a dying Confederate soldier in a poignant scene displaying the mercy of the outlaw contrasted against the brutality of war.

A decade later, Clint Eastwood's own *The Outlaw Josey Wales* (1976), drawing upon the many films about Jesse James, featured the exploits of an unreconstructed Confederate guerrilla that heads West to escape the disgraceful United States cavalry. In the end, he guns down a detachment of the United States Army with the help of a little old lady and her settler family from Kansas. The repudiation of John Ford's position on former Confederates is clear.

In *Unforgiven*, Eastwood further expands on the brutal nature of official law enforcement. When English Bob (Richard Harris) attempts to bring a gun in the town of Big Whiskey, the sheriff, Little Bill (Gene Hackman), beats Bob within an inch of his life and confiscates the gun. The gun control measure, predictably, also fails to prevent the bloodbath at the end of the film. This is a reversal of the gun-control storyline found in the classical Western *Winchester '73* in which Wyatt Earp, sheriff of Dodge City, confiscates the protagonist's gun while he is in town. In this case, gun owners willfully submit and the gun control measures are even shown to be effective in preventing violence within the town. Wyatt Earp does not deliver any vicious beatings in the film.

The contrast between law and order in *Winchester '73* and in *Unforgiven* typifies the change that takes place as the Western genre moves from its classical form to its revisionist form. In the earlier era, willful submission to government authority is assumed for all but violent outlaws. In a later era, however, the brutality of government agents is an ever-present threat.

Abuse of power also appears to be endemic among lawmen within the revisionist Westerns. While some classical Westerns featured crooked lawmen, such portrayals were rarely a commentary on power itself. In a classical Western, the problem of a bad lawman was usually solved by the intervention of a good lawman, while in the revisionist Westerns, power itself is what makes a bad man bad.

The Persistence of Traditional Elements

We cannot assume that negative portrayals of authoritarian government in revisionist Westerns necessarily mean a rehabilitation of the image of bourgeois society in these later films. *The Outlaw Josey Wales* is quite an exception in its magnanimous view of middle-class Kansas settlers who form a close bond with Josey as they build a homestead in the wilderness.

An anti-capitalist and anti-bourgeois bias is obvious in Peckinpah's *The Wild Bunch* (1969) for example, when the opening scenes establish that the outlaws' primary foes are the local railroad conglomerate. The tyrannical and dishonorable railroad men ("We represent the law," they tell us) are contrasted with the honorable killers of the Wild Bunch itself who hold to a code of outlaw honor. The railroad company makes its monstrous nature all the more clear when its hired gunmen open fire on the Wild Bunch, even though a Temperance League parade has wandered into the crosshairs. The resulting bloodbath and the images of bodies of men, women, and children strewn about Main Street serve to further elevate the outlaws above the wicked railroad.

Nameless, faceless business interests are in collusion with the territorial government of New Mexico in *Pat Garrett and*

Billy the Kid (1973). The shadowy businesses are motivated to have Garrett rid them of The Kid because he has become a thorn in the side of the large ranchers who are attempting to consolidate their power in the region. Garrett thinks he's his own man, but in the end, it's revealed that he has not escaped the corrupting influence of corporate America. A man with no name appears in Eastwood's *High Plains Drifter* (1973) to avenge the murder of the late sheriff who discovered that the corporation ruling the town with an iron fist is engaged in illegal mining activities. Naturally, the company will murder to protect its profits. *Pale Rider* (1985), a loose remake of *Shane*, pits small-time miners against large-scale miners with the large mining interests eventually resorting to hiring corrupt marshals to force the small miners off their property.

Sergio Leone appears often to be silent on this issue. While there are groups of men who band together for the express purpose of making money (as in *A Fistful of Dollars* (1964) and *For a Few Dollars More* (1965)), such gangs are portrayed as traditional criminals and not as representatives of business. One exception is Leone's vehemently anti-corporate *Once Upon a Time in the West* (1968) featuring Morton, the railroad baron who will stop at nothing to crush an entrepreneur who has gotten in the railroad's way. As the film progresses, Morton serves as a symbol of Manifest Destiny in addition to being a personification of corporate greed. He repeatedly looks at a painting of the Pacific Ocean and talks at length about how nothing can prevent him from reaching all the way to the Pacific. In a particularly melodramatic touch by Leone, Morton suffers from a rare bone disease so that this symbol of Westward expansion is literally disintegrating from the inside out.

The role of religion is more varied in the revisionist Western than in the classical Western. Some hold to the traditionally hostile view toward religion. Peckinpah in particular is quite down on Christianity. Most of his Westerns feature crazed, Bible-thumping preachers and fundamentalists with words of vengeance on their lips. The Temperance

Union featured in *The Wild Bunch*, obviously a symbol of bourgeois Christianity, is portrayed as innocent but is nevertheless a rather ridiculous group. *Ride the High Country* (1962) and *Pat Garrett and Billy the Kid* both feature actor R.G. Armstrong as a venom-spitting Bible-thumper. In *Pat Garrett and Billy the Kid*, he can barely restrain himself from shooting an unarmed and shackled Billy in the face. In *The Ballad of Cable Hogue* (1970), Hogue's friend, the Reverend Joshua Sloan, is a womanizer and con man who spends his evenings seducing married women.

Clint Eastwood, on the other hand, places supernatural elements into two of his Westerns. *High Plains Drifter* (1973) suggests that the hero is some kind of ghost or avenging angel. He forces the townspeople to literally paint the town red and renames the town "Hell" before burning it to the ground. The "Preacher" (Eastwood), as he is called in *Pale Rider*, appears in the film as a girl reads Scripture: "And behold a pale horse: and his name that sat on him was Death, and Hell followed with him."[80] It is suggested that the Preacher, perhaps murdered by the same men who do the mining company's dirty work, has returned from the dead to even the score. The Preacher wears a collar, hence his name, but trades in his collar for a gun before the showdown. He also seduces another man's fiancée. The Preacher's presence provides some oblique references to Christianity, although the Preacher's origins and his intentions remain quite vague.

Indeed, only in Leone's work do we find any unambiguously positive portrayals of Christianity, couched as a commentary against war. In *The Good, the Bad, and the Ugly*, Blondie and Tuco (Eli Wallach) stumble upon a Franciscan friary where the friars care for the casualties of the war. The head friar makes his contempt for the war known and notes that they care for the dying regardless of the color of the

---

[80] Apocalypse/Revelation 6:8. This same verse is also used in *Tombstone* (1993) to foreshadow the arrival of Wyatt Earp.

uniform they wear. Later, Tuco's lapsed Catholicism and his encounter with his brother, who has become a friar and who is portrayed very sympathetically, are shown to be a source of considerable unease and possible regret for Tuco.

While occasional references to God and the supernatural manage to make their way into some of the later Westerns, it would be a mistake to conclude the standard contempt for religion that dominated the Westerns at mid-century had evaporated in later representatives of the genre. Nor can we say that the fundamental building blocks of the Western as described by Jane Tompkins have disappeared. The central action of the Western still revolves around the gunfighter, and the gunfighter attains his dominant position through a superior command of the primitive landscape where intellectual and economic considerations are of extremely limited importance. Essentially, the gunfighter's behavior remains unchanged, although the context has shifted considerably.

In this respect, Sam Peckinpah's Westerns are very traditional, although his dark vision of the West and his inventive portrayals of violence on film were novel for his time. Peckinpah's Westerns (indeed his films overall) rarely feature women, and the action is generally driven by very violent men who, while vicious, can be quite sympathetic. The gunfighters as shown in *The Wild Bunch*, for example, are men of action and self-sufficient rogues who have no need of religion or women or even civilization. In Peckinpah's films, the gunfighter is destroyed only when civilization catches up with him, and the West is conquered by the modern world.

In *The Ballad of Cable Hogue* (1970), Hogue is killed when an automobile, one of the first he has ever seen, rolls over him and crushes him. The message against modernity is hard to miss.[81] (*The Ballad of Cable Hogue*, however, remains a very

---

[81] *The Ballad of Cable Hogue* is arguably not a Western at all, and has much in common with the *Little House on the Prairie* series in its

unconventional Western, which exalts Hogue as an entrepreneur who uses cunning rather than violence to protect his business interests.) The judgment against modernity is what we would expect from Peckinpah, since we find in his work a significant preoccupation with masculinity and violence in a primitive world, a preoccupation that gives his films much in common with the Westerns of Mann, Hawks, and Ford.

Deadwood, Spontaneous Order, and Progress

Though Westerns have not dominated popular culture in the 20 years since the release of Eastwood's revisionist *Unforgiven* in 1992, numerous Western television series and feature films continue to be made. *Hell on Wheels* and the Kevin Costner vehicle *Open Range* (2003) are relatively high-budget and notable contributions. Perhaps one of the most popular, critically-acclaimed, and groundbreaking Westerns of this period was the HBO series *Deadwood* (2004-2006), featuring the mining town of the same name that once flourished in the Dakota Territory.

In a detailed examination of the series, Paul Cantor identifies the series' highly sympathetic view of spontaneous order. *Deadwood*, according to Cantor, takes the position that ordered human societies can arise independent of the intervention of any established law-enforcement entity, and that those societies are held together by economic self-interest.[82] As we have seen, this is an extremely unusual position for a Western to take. Classical Westerns overwhelmingly take the opposite view and maintain that true order is finally only established with the intervention of a cavalryman, sheriff, or gunman who can pave the way for civilization.

---

treatment of work, violence, and domestic life.
[82] Cantor, "Order Out of the Mud," p. 114.

In *Deadwood*, on the other hand, order arises immediately out of the self-interest of miners and merchants who seek riches and appreciate that peace and a functioning economic system are essential for prosperity.

In the series, Al Swearengen (Ian McShane), the owner of the The Gem, a local saloon and brothel, dominates the town of *Deadwood*. Swearengen, while calculating and brutal, is motivated to maintain as much peace and order in the town as possible for the sake of business. He is also motivated to avoid interference from the federal and territorial governments, and works frequently with local magistrates and business rivals to ensure the political interdependence of *Deadwood* and a relative state of peace. Swearengen's chief antagonist is Seth Bullock (Timothy Olyphant), who eventually becomes sheriff of Deadwood yet fails to ensure order. In typical style for a Western, the central villain in *Deadwood* is a mining magnate who manipulates political authorities and engages in other forms of fraud and corruption to the detriment of the town.

Noting that *Deadwood* is "as close to philosophical as popular culture ever gets," Cantor views *Deadwood* as an examination of the philosophies of Thomas Hobbes and John Locke. As far as the origins of order are concerned, Locke approaches the question by asking (as paraphrased by Cantor):

> Can human beings spontaneously arrive at rules that make possible and facilitate their productive social interaction, or are they dependent on the central authority of the state to create and enforce law and only thereby to make life in society feasible?[83]

Locke's eventual answer to this question is "yes" while Hobbes' answer is an emphatic "no." Hobbes, who famously

---

[83] *Ibid.*, p. 115.

contends in *Leviathan* (1651) that life is "nasty, brutish, and short," provides the overarching political and moral framework for the classical Western. In Ford's cavalry films, the U.S. Cavalry must clean out the Indians and impose order, end trade with Indians, and generally provide the blessings of government-imposed peace. In *The Tin Star* and *High Noon* the sheriff imposes order on a chaotic and disorganized population, and in *Liberty Valance*, "progress" is defined as the gunning down of outlaws followed by the arrival of the nation-state and all its trappings. *Deadwood* repudiates all of this, Cantor claims, and describes Deadwood as a place where "there was order and no law whatsoever."[84]

It is significant that the message of Deadwood reflects the classical liberalism that is so characteristic of Locke's philosophy and is a key component of later bourgeois liberalism. We find yet again that it is a revisionist Western that takes a sympathetic view of the bourgeois liberal values of laissez-faire markets and small decentralized government. The classical Western, on the other hand, supposedly representative of traditional American values, reflects instead an authoritarian Hobbesian view.

Not only are economic interests of men like Al Swearengen and the miners essential in holding together the political order, but it also serves to domesticate the men to an extent and force them to set aside violence in favor of peace and collaboration. According to Cantor:

> In *Deadwood*, commerce is the chief force that works to produce order without law. Above all, it seems to be the only force that can get the alpha males to set aside their differences, give up their fighting to the death, and work together for their mutual benefit.[85]

---

[84] David Milch quoted in Cantor, "Order Out of the Mud," p. 115.
[85] *Ibid.*, p. 124.

In Hobbes' view, this sort of collaboration is impossible since in his state of nature, "human beings will simply start killing each other, and only the Leviathan State can stop them."[86]

This is obviously not true in the vision of *Deadwood* however, in which the local merchants and miners want order and are willing to band together in a variety of complex and creative ways to do it, short of forming a permanent government.

There is eventually an "official" representative of law enforcement in *Deadwood*. Seth Bullock, the former federal-marshal-turned-sheriff of Deadwood, ends up offering little to the town, however, and fails to understand the delicate and skillful methods used by Swearengen to protect the peace and independence of the community. As Cantor describes it: "the intellectual complexity of the series is evident in the way that Swearengen, the criminal, turns out to be for order in the community, while Bullock, the lawman, turns out to be a force for disorder."[87] Bullock lacks the self-control and long-term thinking that Swearengen possesses, and this impels Bullock to act in ways that eventually work against the interests of the local social and economic order.

Few of the characters in Deadwood display what might be termed heroic behavior, and in typical fashion for a revisionist Western, the protagonists are more anti-heroes than anything else. In yet another twist on the classical Western, and in keeping with the overall repudiation of classical Western values, Al Swearengen, the foul-mouthed "criminal" of the town, turns out the be the closest thing the town has to an effective representative of bourgeois liberal values. It's Swearengen who exhibits fortitude, patience, and an ability to plan ahead, invest, and look out for the good of the community. It's this brothel owner who comes closer to

---

[86] *Ibid.*, p. 122.
[87] *Ibid.*, p. 124.

exemplifying the values of bourgeois America than any cavalryman, sheriff, or wandering gunfighter of the era of classical Westerns.

The relationship between the town of Deadwood and the territorial and national governments is also very different from that found in classical Westerns. In Ford's cavalry films, *Winchester '73*, and *The Man from Laramie*, for example, the cavalry itself is a symbol of the assumed civilizing effect of the United States government that makes the settling of the frontier possible. A central theme in classical Westerns in general is that the story of the West is one of progress toward modern civilization. This is often communicated with a wistful nostalgia, as in *Shane* and *My Darling Clementine*, but the march toward civilization is assumed to be inevitable and ultimately advantageous to American society.

Deadwood, as with many revisionist Westerns, takes a different approach, but *Deadwood* takes the critique of centralized government and its commentary on progress to a more sophisticated level than is normally seen in Westerns. Both *The Wild Bunch* and *Once Upon a Time in the West* look upon the end of frontier life as the end of something good. In *The Wild Bunch*, and *Pat Garrett and Billy the Kid*, an older world of gunfighter honor is being lost to a corrupt modernism. In *Once Upon a Time in the West*, the gunfighter is almost literally buried by the railroad as industrialization replaces the way of the gun. Here we find all the elements of nostalgic primitivism in which the masculine gunmen are replaced by a more effeminate and complex society, which in some ways resembles the industrialized society of bourgeois liberal America.

Deadwood departs even from these lingering elements of the Western and posits that something far more important than masculinity or gunfighter honor is lost in the march of progress. According to Cantor:

Elements of the Western myth of progress are present in *Deadwood*, especially in season 3, when outside forces truly begin to transform the town. But [series creator David] Milch evaluates the transformation quite differently, and refuses to view it simply as progress. More than any other Western I know, *Deadwood* dwells upon what is lost when a town makes the transition to civilization and becomes part of the nation-state. What is lost is freedom.[88]

In *Deadwood*, territorial and national officials are viewed as thieves and bureaucrats whose primary interest is stealing from the Indians, and, when they can get away with it, from the white civilians also. "They're too busy stealing to study human nature" one character remarks, while a local saloon owner during the second season declares:

Who of us here didn't know what government was before we came? Wasn't half our purpose coming to get shed of the cocksucker? And here it comes again – to do what's in its nature – to lie to us, and confuse us, and steal what we came to by toil and being lucky just once in our fuckin' lives. And we gonna be surprised by that, boys, government being government?[89]

Continuing a general trend in revisionist Westerns, agents of the government in *Deadwood* not only steal, but are also enablers for criminals and thugs who function to make the lives of whites and Indians even more miserable.

Deadwood is perhaps the apotheosis of the revisionist Western in its view of the central government. The Westerns of Peckinpah, for example, paint government agents as simultaneously incompetent and menacing. Amos Dundee of

---

[88] Ibid., p. 132.
[89] Ibid., p. 135.

Major Dundee is an agent of chaos on the frontier while the foolish and inept American lawmen who take on the Wild Bunch are stooges for a corrupt regime. The warmongers of the central government in *The Good, The Bad, and the Ugly* spread murder and discord while the marshals in Eastwood's *Pale Rider* come to drive small businessmen off their land and enforce the rule of might over right. Meanwhile, the outlaw Josey Wales flees a triumphant and murderous nation-state formed out of the ruins of the bloody Civil War.

In *Deadwood*, we learn that these tales of woe brought by government in other Westerns are not isolated cases, but are in the very nature of the nation-state itself. If progress consists of the march toward the consolidation of the American state over the "lawless" frontier, then progress is something the people of Deadwood can do without.

This is, of course, a very different view of progress than what is presented in John Ford's *The Man Who Shot Liberty Valance*. Like many Westerns of the 1950s and early 60s, (such as *Cheyenne Autumn* and *Shane*) the end of the Wild West is presented with a melancholy tone, but *Liberty Valance* nonetheless endorses the triumph of progress in a number of ways. First of all, it is assumed that statehood for the territory is a good thing. We know this because the villainous ranchers, in league with the barbaric Liberty Valance, oppose statehood, and newspaperman Dutton Peabody is even savagely beaten by Valance (as a service to the ranchers) for supporting statehood.

The killing of Valance then paves the way for statehood, and Stoddard, the assumed killer of Valance, is made a senator of the new state. The film views all of these developments with approval. It then goes an extra step and endorses the use of the Noble Lie to attain statehood, and, presumably, progress.[90]

---

[90] Plato endorsed the use of the Noble Lie to maintain order over the presumably ignorant masses, and in this case, the reality of

As Stoddard begins to doubt himself, having built his success on a lie, the film makes pretenses toward being subversive by momentarily calling into question the legitimacy of progress attained through deception. Ultimately, however, the film concludes that the truth is best glossed over and swept under the rug and that any means to achieve progress is acceptable because progress is both beneficial and inevitable.

In *Liberty Valance*, the truth is that civilization is made possible by the frontier gunfighter. The lie is that civilization can be attained through men like Ransom Stoddard. If the lie is necessary to attain civilization, so be it, but the truth will remain the truth. Progress, specifically in this case, so valuable as to be obtained though any means necessary, is the establishment of a modern, bureaucratic, and centralized government and all the advantages that brings.

That *Deadwood*'s message is a departure from the message of progress contained in *Liberty Valance* would be an understatement. In the classical Westerns, the nation-state is indispensable thanks to its cavalry, its marshals, and its eventual establishment of official law and order. This is the march of progress in the Western, and a progress that led to the modern United States, which in 1962 was perceived by movie audiences as the very symbol and embodiment of the free world.

By the late 1960s, the view of the American nation-state promoted by the classical Western had fallen on hard times. The frontier in film had become a different place, and was now plagued by corrupt government officials checked only by dying and irrelevant heroes whose days were numbered. Yet even in this new West, the old conventions of primitivism, redemptive violence, and villainous capitalists remains largely

---

Doniphon's killing of Liberty Valance helped make progress possible. Thus, the film asserts that deception is preferable to truth.

in tact. By the 1990s, however, even the gunfighter would face the doubts of filmmakers.

"Something To Do with Death"

In the historical West, gunfighters were marginal figures, but in the cinematic West, they are everything—the axis upon which the Western spins. Thus a Western about the gunfighter, as opposed to a Western that *features* gunfighters, is really a Western about Westerns. Two Westerns stand out as being particularly effective in this regard: Leone's *Once Upon a Time in the West* and Eastwood's *Unforgiven*. In both of these films, the Western comes as close as possible to repudiating itself while still retaining the qualities of being a Western. In these late revisionist Westerns, the gunfighter is no longer essential. Domestic bourgeois values exist in tension with the gunfighter ethic, and the outcome is quite different than what we would expect from a traditional Western.

Once Upon a Time in the West was Leone's last Western. Leone believed the Western's days were numbered, and he sought to produce a film that he believed would serve as both an elegy for the visual legacy of the Western and as a critique on the centrality of death and violence.

Early in the film, Brett McBain, an entrepreneur, has purchased the only plot of land with water for miles around. This forces the railroad to use his water for the men and the locomotives, putting McBain in a position to make a lot of money at the railroad's expense. The railroad's owner, Morton, concludes that he will simply have McBain and his family murdered. He does just this, and when the railroad's hired gunmen shoot an unarmed little boy at point-blank range, it drives home the brutality of the frontier in cinema. Unfortunately for the railroad, however, they have not killed McBain's new wife, who arrives shortly thereafter on the train.

Jill McBain (Claudia Cardinale) quickly takes control of her late husband's assets and faces down the railroad. She does this through a mixture of intellectual and sexual guile by which she manipulates Frank (Henry Fonda), the railroad's most dangerous gunman. Jill never arms herself with a gun, for she obviously can't outgun her enemies. Instead, she coldly calculates how she will take advantage of her enemies' weaknesses, playing the company and its hired guns against each other. She is assisted by a nameless gunfighter (Charles Bronson) who constantly plays a harmonica, and a romantic outlaw named Cheyenne (Jason Robards). Frank, a sadistic killer who guns down women and children with pleasure, only spares Jill so he can sexually assault her, or so he thinks. Jill, however, is not fazed by Frank, and as she makes clear to Cheyenne, not even Frank can stop her from making her late-husband's investments pay off.

Visually, the film contrasts Jill and the gunfighters through the McBain estate itself, a large, sturdy house built to function both as residence and whistle stop. The film establishes the house as a reliable fixture of the physical and moral landscape, while the gunfighters wander the land, coming from nowhere and heading nowhere. Jill makes plans for the future while the gunfighters hunt each other in endless chases and showdowns.

This juxtaposition of stalwart Jill and the ephemeral gunfighters produces a situation which illustrates that in Leone's vision, those with guns know how to unleash much violence, but they haven't a good idea about how to use it effectively. Whether or not Cheyenne and Harmonica are essential in saving Jill's ownership of the train station remains ambiguous, for ultimately, Frank and Morton destroy each other after a series of double-crosses. All Jill has to do is endure their crude attempts at intimidation until the villains ultimately self-destruct.

As most Westerns do, *Once Upon a Time in the West* builds to a final showdown. The showdown, between Harmonica and Frank, has nothing to do with Jill, for the railroad has already been neutralized. The showdown is a personal matter of revenge for Harmonica who has been searching for Frank for years in order to kill him for crimes he committed decades earlier. During this final showdown, Jill's attraction to Harmonica becomes clear, but Cheyenne talks her out of pursuing a relationship with him, telling her: "People like that have something inside — something to do with death."

Jill, the symbol of the settled bourgeois life, can never maintain a relationship with the gunfighter, because the two lifestyles cannot be reconciled. The gunfighter is not a complement to the bourgeois life, nor is he its protector. He is instead either irrelevant or damaging to the settlement of the West, wild and prone to self-destruction. As the film draws to a close, Harmonica and Cheyenne ride away from Jill's estate to die, forgotten and useless in the dust.

Dedicated to Sergio Leone, Clint Eastwood's *Unforgiven* takes Leone's critique of the gunfighter and presents a far darker and much more devastating deconstruction of the gunfighter and everything he stands for. Unforgiven opens in a brothel. But this is not one of the well-lit, ribald brothels of the classical Western. Inside, a cowboy is cutting up a whore who has laughed at his miniscule genitals. His assault ends with the sheriff Little Bill arriving with his deputies and demanding that the cowboy and his partner compensate not the woman who's been cut up, but the brothel owner for destruction of his "property." The sheriff's obvious disregard for the concept of self-ownership and his alarmingly light punishment leads the whores to pool their money to hire a bounty hunter.

Enter William Munny (Eastwood), a vicious outlaw who we are repeatedly told has killed women and children, and is a former Civil War guerrilla. Munny had turned away from gunfighting while under the influence of his wife Claudia, a "respectable" woman who married Munny against her mother's wishes. Yet by the time the news of the whores' bounty reaches Munny, Claudia has died and Munny has fallen on hard times. Munny is recruited by The Schofield

Kid, a youth who talks too much and obviously wants to make a name for himself with a few killings. Munny accepts the job largely out of his desperate need for money (he has two children), and he brings on his old partner Ned (Morgan Freeman) for one last job.

As the film unfolds, Munny repeatedly refers to what Claudia would have wanted from him. "She cured me of drinkin' and wickedness," he tells Ned. He's only doing this for the money, and to set things right for what the cowboy did to the whore. Claudia haunts the film every step of the way, and even in death she is an enduring symbol of domesticity and peace. It was she who turned Munny away from the life of the gun. It was she who built a house with him, had children with him, and worked a farm with him. Now, by accepting this job, he is risking repudiating everything she ever taught him.

Through most of the film, Munny holds fast to what Claudia would have wanted. He invokes her name like a mantra, and, unlike his partners, he doesn't patronize the brothel or drink any whiskey. He's in town to make some money and return to his children. Unfortunately, Munny runs into Little Bill, the sheriff who has scarcely any less experience in gunning men down than Munny does. Indeed, it may be that the only difference between Little Bill and Munny is that Little Bill wears a badge.

Little Bill's viciousness was well established earlier in the film when he administered a savage beating to English Bob (Richard Harris), a gunfighter who had attempted to bring a pistol into town against Little Bill's regulations.[91] After the beating, Bill shares with Bob's biographer the secrets of being a gunfighter. In this conversation, Bill essentially deconstructs the myth of the gunfighter, pointing out that a fast draw and the other legends of the dime novels of the time had very

---

[91] This may be a reference to the gun ban in force in Dodge City in Mann's *Winchester '73*.

103

little to do with reality. In real life, Bill tells us, winning a gunfight is about getting the drop on your opponent, taking careful aim, and shooting him down. The showdowns of myth are ridiculous, Bill tells us.

At this point, Bill is just confirming what Munny has been telling us throughout the entire film. The Schofield Kid continually grills Munny, seeking to learn his secrets to winning gunfights; yet Munny himself isn't even sure how he came out of so many gunfights on top. He attributes most of it to luck: "I've always been lucky when it came to killin' folks," he says, and he owns that he doesn't remember much of it because he was drunk most of the time. According to Munny himself, there isn't much that's courageous or interesting about being a gunfighter. Thus Claudia is confirmed as Munny's salvation and as his rescuer from a world of drunkenness and murder.

Munny feels the pull of the domestic life through his memories of Claudia, but we know that Little Bill also feels this pull. We learn that Little Bill is building a house as a domestic refuge from the violence of his job. The house is poorly built, the roof leaks, and "there's not a straight angle in the place." Little Bill's shoddy house sets up a second symbol of bourgeois domesticity set against the life of the gunfighter. Just as Munny cannot simultaneously honor Claudia's memory and gun down the cowboys for the bounty, neither can Little Bill build a neat little bourgeois life for himself at the same time he is raining blows upon every man who dares question his authority.[92]

After Munny, Ned, and the Kid kill the offending cowboy and his innocent friend for the bounty, Ned is

---

[92] John Ford uses the device of house building in *The Man Who Shot Liberty Valance*. Tom Doniphon is adding a bedroom onto his house in expectation of marrying the heroine. Later, after his status as a gunfighter is confirmed, Doniphon gets drunk and accidently burns down his own house.

captured and tortured to death by Little Bill. The final epiphany for Munny comes when he learns of Ned's death at the hands of Little Bill, and Munny takes his first drink of whiskey since his marriage to Claudia. Munny returns to town to shoot down Little Bill and every member of his posse, even shooting some of them in the back. Little Bill, dying on the floor, declares to Munny, "I don't deserve this, to die like this. I was building a house." Little Bill's appeal to justice is not that he was a good man or a good sheriff, but that he was building a house, the symbol of everything that the gunfighter is not.

Critical analyses of *Unforgiven* are common, and a common conclusion among them is that the film is a commentary on the futility of violence. This is certainly true, and we know this from Eastwood himself. The film begins with a non-lethal assault on a woman and ends with a bloodbath. By the end of the film, the bounty itself, which had precipitated so much killing, appears excessive, for in fact, the whore's scars from the original assault have healed and are already faded by the time the final showdown commences.

Some have claimed that the film's coda, which tells us that after he returns home, Munny becomes a businessman in San Francisco, proves that Munny's return to gunfighting bore much fruit. Yet we know that earlier in the film, Munny had confronted his own mortality. He had seen "the angel of death," was terrified, and had seen the face of his wife, "all covered in worms." Why does the film include this? It certainly doesn't do much to convince us that Munny, after getting drunk and shooting a few men in the back, will be living happily ever after.

And while the role of violence is a central theme, the presence of Claudia's memory and Little Bill's house serve to illustrate the alternative for the gunfighter. It is the peaceful bourgeois life of the settlers. But neither Little Bill nor Munny is capable of living this life. They are condemned to the shiftless life of the gun with no wife, no home, and nothing but a life of endless combat and death. The connection to *Once Upon a Time in the West* is clear, for Cheyenne and Harmonica were likewise incapable of settling down. They were committed to the life of the gunfighter, and like the lives of Little Bill and Munny, the life of the gunfighter is sterile. They create nothing and destroy everything. They cannot sustain themselves and ultimately ride to the horizon as ruined men to die.

A Victorian Western: *Little House on the Prairie*

In 1930, Rose Wilder Lane, a successful essayist and novelist, encouraged her mother, Laura Ingalls Wilder, to write an autobiography as part of a plan to help Wilder gain a stream of income from her writing. Wilder at that time had published little, and her daughter Lane, who had already met with much writing success during the 1920s, had spent several years during the twenties with her mother and father in Missouri helping her mother develop her writing skills.

With Lane's help, Wilder's autobiography, which was repeatedly rejected by publishers, was eventually reworked into fictional form and became a series of books known today as the *Little House on the Prairie* series.

While Rose Wilder Lane is still remembered for her highly influential libertarian essay, *The Discovery of Freedom* (1943), it is Lane's mother Laura Ingalls Wilder who is today the more widely-read author due to the *Little House* series of books and the television series and made-for-TV movies based on the books.[93] While the books themselves have long been most popular among school children, the television show reached a national audience of all ages as a prime-time fixture on NBC for nine seasons from 1974 to 1983, and continues in syndication on several cable channels today.

---

[93] Rose Wilder Lane, *The Discovery of Freedom* (New York, NY: The John Day Co., 1943)

While thought to be a Western by many viewers due to its frontier setting, *Little House on the Prairie*, as we shall see, departs drastically from the form of the classical Westerns in its lack of gun violence and in its central emphasis on themes of commerce, family, women, children, education, and religious faith.

If Jane Tompkins is correct, and the Western thoroughly repudiates the themes of the middle-class bourgeois novel of the late nineteenth-century, we find a partial restoration of that literature in the *Little House* series.

Although the series is about the settlement of the American frontier, gone is the gunfighter as savior of the townsfolk, and gone is the centrality of violence in general. The series instead repeatedly focuses on the importance of commerce in settling the frontier.

The series centers on the Ingalls family, headed by Charles Ingalls (Michael Landon) and his wife, Caroline (Karen Grassle), and their three daughters. Unlike the typical Western in which women and children are only marginal characters, the lives of the female characters, and in particular the female children, are of central importance to the drama. Charles Ingalls, intended to be a model of masculinity in the series, rarely uses a gun. He is most often seen performing domestic duties as a husband and father and engaging in commerce.

Domestic settings, women, children, shops and shopkeepers, schoolhouses, and churches are all frequent settings for the series. In the world of Walnut Grove, Minnesota, where the series mostly takes place, there would be no room for an authoritarian sheriff like Ben Owens of *The Tin Star*, a violent bounty hunter like Howard Kemp from *The Naked Spur*, or a drifter like the protagonist of *Shane*.

Law and order in Walnut Grove is maintained not primarily by a sheriff or by any formal law enforcement officials but by the townspeople who work together to address conflicts and crimes that occur within the town. Most episodes feature family conflicts and drama that stems from challenges presented by earning a living on the frontier or from the physical environment.

In the episode "The Creeper of Walnut Grove," foodstuffs are being stolen from the townspeople, who react with dismay, but deal with the thefts in a restrained fashion. In response, Laura Ingalls and a friend take it upon themselves to catch the thief using skills they have learned from reading detective novels. The thief turns out to be a young man who hopes to attend medical school but whose father has suffered a debilitating heart attack and is unable to make a living. No gunfight ensues.

Sometimes the series features relations between whites and Indians, although these episodes often emphasize the fact that both sides are highly motivated to avoid violence. In the episode "Freedom Flight," a group of Indians who must migrate from their government-appointed reservation, which is on barren land, enter the town to seek the help of a physician. The whites are distrustful but wish to avoid violence, in spite of the problematic rabble-rousing of one racist member of the town. Dialogue and conflict-resolution skills are employed to avoid a bloodbath.

This theme of Indian-white relations is also clear in the original series pilot. The Ingalls family, which has recently re-located to the Kansas Territory, meets the local Indians in numerous tension-filled encounters, although violence is always avoided. The family is eventually driven off the land, but by the U.S. government and not by the Indians. The few local whites they encounter are generally helpful and certainly not menacing.

The episode "He Was Only Twelve" is one of the few episodes that features truly dangerous criminals. In it, Charles Ingalls's adopted son James is shot and severely injured when he walks in on a bank robbery in progress. The criminals escape. A lack of available law enforcement forces Charles and Isaiah (Mr.) Edwards to hunt the robbers on their own. The two men eventually catch up with the robbers, and Charles, filled with rage, nearly kills one of them. After intervention from Edwards, Charles thinks better of it, and the robbers are subdued and turned over to the authorities to stand trial.

Obviously, the narrative here is quite different from the sorts of conflicts found in classical Westerns. In this case, the instruments of law and order are amateur gunmen, and when the climax of the chase comes, Charles and Edwards refrain from using deadly force even though they could have easily justified doing so.

Aside from the rare violent criminal, the overwhelming majority of people encountered by the Ingalls family and their neighbors are non-threatening and mostly concerned with earning a living, raising their children, and finding some moments of leisure. There are numerous cases in which scripture is quoted in an approving way, and, unlike the classical Western, which cheapens dialogue, education, and economic profit, such concerns are invariably treated with approval in the series.[94] A great number of scenes take place inside the general store or in the schoolhouse, and, while such locations would only be featured in the classical Western as part of a prelude to a gunfight, schoolrooms and shops are the central theatre of the human drama for the people of Walnut Grove.

One could reasonably argue that the *Little House* series differs so significantly from classical Western films like the post-war films of John Ford because *Little House* was made for television viewing by families while the films of Mann, Ford and Hawks were feature films for adult audiences.

Television Westerns do tend to be slightly different in tone, and the intensity and graphic nature of violence in

---

[94] Charles Ingalls is portrayed as a man who attempts to live up to a Christian standard. Sometimes his wife will quote Scripture in order to make a point about household chores or the important role of women in the family, at which point Charles will usually capitulate to her demands.

television Westerns of the 1950s and 60s is toned down somewhat from what one might find in the feature films of Ford and Mann. The story lines are more varied, given the needs of filming dozens, if not hundreds, of episodes for a single series. The need to vary story lines results in more story lines that reflect corrupt government officials, while few such story lines were found in major motion pictures of the fifties and early 60s. Programs such as *Wagon Train* (1957-1962) and *Rawhide* (1959-1965), for example, rely less on established law enforcement than a typical 50s film, although *The Lone Ranger* is a de facto Texas Ranger who acts alone. Family themes were more common as well, since several main characters in *The Rifleman* and *Bonanza* were family relations.

The overall content and structure remains largely similar however. Killings are a frequent event in *Rawhide, Bonanza* and *The Rifleman*; and the *Wagon Train* frequently employs Indian massacres as a plot device. Typical story lines in TV Westerns of the 50s and 60s include kidnappings, range wars, and numerous varieties of homicide. The usual assumptions about the chaotic nature of the frontier are repeated, as in the pilot to the *Lone Ranger* television series in which the announcer states "here beyond the reach of law and order, 'might was right.'"[95]

Bonanza, a long-running television Western that occupied prime-time scheduling very similar to that of *Little House on the Prairie*, helps to illustrate just how much *Little House* differed from the typical Western set-up.

The main cast of *Bonanza*, for instance, is completely composed of men. The series follows the exploits of the Cartwright family, which owns the Ponderosa Ranch on the California-Nevada border. The family, however, has no living female members. Following the model established in *Red River*, this family patriarch has all male children without the

---

[95] *The Lone Ranger* (1949-1957), Episode 1, Season 1, "Enter the Lone Ranger."

inconvenience of a wife. There is family conflict, but it is all between men, and the drama frequently stems from the presence of interlopers, criminals, cavalrymen, Indians, gamblers, and other threats to the family and the ranch. Gunplay is frequent while the presence of children, woman, and schools are infrequently made known.

The setting of the series, on a ranch controlled by a powerful family separated from day-to-day town life, is far more reminiscent of the classical Western than anything found in the *Little House* series. The difference in tone and violence between the Little House series and the classical Westerns that came before it cannot be explained simply by the difference in media.

In its treatment of some contemporary issues such as race and bigotry, the *Little House* series shows signs of being updated for a 1970s audience. But, in general, the series holds to the themes explored in the original books written by Wilder.

In this essay, I have contended that the classical Western discounts and undermines nineteenth-century bourgeois liberal values of free commerce, small government, liberalism, family, and religious faith.

The contrast between the *Little House* series and the classical Westerns illustrates just how great is the difference between the typical Western and frontier fiction which features family life and commerce apart from violence.

The *Little House* series reminds us that the Western formula is not the only way of addressing the American frontier through fiction. The *Little House* stories offer an alternate model, as do the frontier stories of Willa Cather, for example.

In spite of a thoroughly different focus from that provided by the Western, the *Little House* series does not question the value of the Westward expansion of American civilization. It simply contends that the expansion was far less violent and chaotic than what is shown in the classical Western. Wilder's books, and the *Little House* television series as well, exhibit a substantial amount of optimism about Westward expansion and sympathy for the settlers themselves. *Little House* is not a revisionist Western in the model of *The Wild Bunch* or *High Plains Drifter.*

Coupled with an examination of the importance of commerce and local self-reliance, the focus on the virtues of nineteenth-century American frontier society found in the Little House series bears the marks of the influence of Rose Wilder Lane.

The true extent of Lane's involvement in the writing of the Little House stories has long been debated, but John E. Miller, author of *Laura Ingalls Wilder and Rose Wilder Lane: Authorship, Place, Time, and Culture*, proposes that Lane's involvement was as much more than "collaborator," but still less than "composite author."[96] It is significant that Lane, who is known for her support of laissez-faire economics and small and decentralized government, would push a much different view of the frontier than what is found in the typical Western with its traditional themes. According to Miller, in working on the Little House books, Lane "would follow the practice she had established in [her novel] Let the Hurricane Roar and her Missouri book–injecting doses of conservative political ideology...for the benefit of her readers."[97] Miller displays an inexact understanding of Lane's political ideology here, but he is likely suggesting that Lane was injecting her own Lockean brand of liberalism into the Little House stories.[98]

---

[96] John E. Miller, *Laura Ingalls Wilder and Rose Wilder Lane: Authorship, Place, Time and Culture* (Columbia, MO: University of Missouri Press, 2008), p. 35.

[97] *Ibid.*, p. 126.

[98] Miller refers to Lane's ideology as "conservative" although it is doubtful that Lane would self-identify as conservative. Lane is more recognized as a libertarian, and was not closely affiliated with the nationalistic and militantly anti-communist movement that came to be known as the American Conservative movement. For

Lane's bourgeois liberal philosophy is also reflected in the social structure of the American frontier, as featured in the *Little House* stories and series. Unlike the classical Western, which creates a myth of a totally self-sufficient gunfighter or military man who is largely untouchable and lives apart from civilized society, the *Little House* series emphasizes the need for community action, education, cooperation, and family, which arise, incidentally, out of an order established by the settlers independent of any powerful government institution.

As perhaps a final repudiation of the Western genre and its roots in nostalgic primitivism, The *Little House* series of books re-defines masculinity along much different lines. According to Jim Powell, writing in *The Triumph of Liberty*:

> Pa was the great hero of the stories. For example, On the Banks of Plum Creek told how, after locusts devoured the wheat and hay which he had grown in Minnesota, he twice walked more than 200 miles east in his old patched boots, to earn money harvesting other people's crops. On another occasion, walking home from town, he was caught in a sudden blizzard and lost his way, but he survived three days in a hole until the blizzard was over. Again and again, Pa renewed everybody's spirits when he picked up his fiddle and filled their home with music.[99]

In the classical Western, virtue is defined by the competent use of coercive power, while in the Little House

more, see Brian Doherty's *Radicals for Capitalism*, (Public Affairs Press, 2008) or Justin Raimondo's *Reclaiming the American Right*, (Intercollegiate Studies Institute, 2008).
[99] Jim Powell, *The Triumph of Liberty*, (New York, NY: The Free Press, 2000), p. 232.

stories, as in the television series, virtue is defined by one's ability to earn a living, make music, and persevere though physical hardships.

Powell attributed these themes in the *Little House* series to Lane's libertarian leanings and to her sizable influence over the writing of the books.

In a 2012 article in *The New Yorker* titled "A Libertarian House on the Prairie," Judith Thurman noted this emphasis on community in Lane's work and recalled that it was a source of conflict with Lane's contemporary and occasional associate Ayn Rand. Thurman states that Rand took exception with Lane's denial that unrestrained self-interest was beneficial to society.[100]

Taking for granted that Lane was instrumental in the thematic construction of the Little House stories, Thurman concludes by observing that one can "hear the congenial echo of Lane's polemics in [the *Little House* stories], though tempered by something more humane...[t]hey exalt rugged self-reliance, but as Lane suggested rather plaintively in her argument with Rand, the pioneers would have perished (in greater numbers than they did) had they embraced the philosophy of every man for himself."

The *Little House* series provides a glimpse into what frontier-themed film and fiction looks like when open to bourgeois themes of commerce, family, and self-government. Far from pretending that women did not exist on the frontier, or that crime was rampant there, the series instead focuses on the more mundane challenges of daily life, while nevertheless playing up conflicts within the town for dramatic effect. Crime did exist, of course, and this was often dealt with through the intervention of private citizens who sought the

---

[100] Judith Thurman, "A Libertarian House on the Prairie." *The New Yorker*, August 17, 2012, https://www.newyorker.com/books/page-turner/a-libertarian-house-on-the-prairie

least-violent solutions possible. Militarism, Indian massacres, abusive capitalists, and spineless villagers are as marginal in Little House as they are front and center in the typical classical Westerns.

As with frontiersman Charles Goodnight's frontier film *Old Texas*, the Little House series, written by a woman of the historical frontier, does not rely on a myth in which the nation-state and its literary stand-in, the gunfighter, are necessary for order. Order was formed in Walnut Grove out of the self-interest and long-term planning and cooperative efforts of citizens. In Walnut Grove, a world with few kidnappings, massacres, robberies, and killings, a gunfighter would find little to do except settle down and worry about making money and having children like everyone else.

Little House doesn't directly compete with classical Westerns, of course, because it does not fill the same niche. There is none of the sweeping sense of epic adventure, nor is there the cathartic violence of the final showdown. Such stories have always been popular in fiction and will likely always continue to be so, but it is odd that their defenders continue to associate such adventures with the far more mundane, commercial, and domestic values of classical liberalism.

Conclusion

Writing in the early 1960s, Frank Chodorov, the highly-influential libertarian and proponent of laissez-faire capitalism, declared in a light-hearted but sincere column that he watches Westerns, probably due to a "bad case of 'juvenilism.'"[101] Chodorov goes on to assert that Westerns are "singularly devoid of 'messages'" and that there is "nothing in

---

[101] Frank Chodorov, "I Watch Westerns," Mises Institute, Last modified February 2011, https://mises.org/library/i-watch-westerns.

115

them but entertainment." He also claims that the characters in Westerns "fend for themselves under all manner of adverse conditions," ask "for help from nobody," and that "nobody preaches 'togetherness.'" "Everybody is "sturdy, self-reliant, and self-responsible," says Chodorov, and he concludes that the Western is so pleasurable because it repudiates all the humbuggery of his day.

In many of these statements, Chodorov is demonstrably wrong. Obviously, the Western can't be both devoid of "messages" while simultaneously encouraging self reliance and plain-talking common sense as Chodorov imagines. The genre is perhaps one of the most message-laden genres extant due to its status as a type of American origin story. There's much more in a Western than mere entertainment.

Additionally, so much of the genre is dominated by weak citizens in need of protection from battle-hardened gunfighters that it would be wholly inaccurate to describe the characters of Westerns as people who fend for themselves while asking for help "from nobody." One of the central conceits of numerous Western films is the need for help from a gunfighter, who sometimes is a private citizen but is just as often a military officer or lawman. In the post-World War II, Cold War World, the audience knew who the gunfighter was. He was the American state, and he had a big gun.

From the farmers in *Shane* to the townsfolk of *True Grit* or *The Man who Shot Liberty Valance*, the settlers of the old frontier were hardly self-reliant. They needed the gunman, and they needed him badly. The heroes of *Two Rode Together* and *High Noon* preach togetherness while the townsfolk look out for their own petty interests.

Additionally, the Western served to reinforce so much of what Chodorov would have considered the humbuggery of his day. Chodorov specifically opposed the militaristic anti-communism of the Cold War, yet the Western, as demonstrated repeatedly by Engelhardt in *The End of Victory Culture*, was one of the chief elements of popular culture that reinforced American prejudices about the justice of prosecuting the Cold War through superior firepower. The massacres of treacherous, back-stabbing Indians in film helped to justify the widespread killing of Japanese civilians during the Second World War, while the role of the frontier gunman as peacemaker illustrated the need for a strong American state in the "anarchic" international world that included Soviet communism.[102]

As a defender of classical liberalism and learned man of letters, if Chodorov had somehow been magically transported to the world of the classical Western (which is unlikely since Jewish characters are virtually non-existent in classical Westerns), he would certainly not have been cast as a Sheriff Chance or a Kirby Yorke. Instead, he would be portrayed as a Ransom Stoddard or one of the cowering townsfolk lacking the important skills necessary to be of any value on the frontier. He would be depicted as prejudiced or perhaps unappreciative toward the gunfighter who protects him from a violent and horrible death. In the end, the Chodorov character might finally recognize that yes, civilization is made possible by the U.S. Army, the man with the badge or by the silent and strong former outlaw who paves the way for prosperity and freedom on the frontier.

Chodorov's enthusiasm for Westerns illustrates the widespread misconception among many of its defenders regarding the value system promoted by the genre.

Far from being an exemplar of the bourgeois liberal values of an earlier America, the Western inveighs against free-markets and defends the power of the nation-state. It attacks domestic life, intellectuals, Christian civilization, and peace.

---

[102] Engelhardt links the common presence of "extermination" narratives in Westerns of the period to the need to justify the war on Japanese civilians. The Japanese were linked to the Indians in wartime and post-wartime popular culture in order to illustrate the incorrigible and alien nature of Japanese society.

Far from preserving so-called traditional American values, it instead seeks to overturn the value system of the nineteenth century Americans who actually settled the frontier.

The Western repudiates the Victorian bourgeois culture and literature of the nineteenth century by offering a very different vision. This vision reached its peak with the post-war classical Westerns in which the people of the frontier, and by extension the audience, were given a choice between the way of the gun and total subjugation. As a Cold War fable, the Western at mid-century took the elements present in the early Westerns and expanded them to their most developed form in which the frontier is a violent and forbidding place made habitable only with the power of the gun and the gunfighter.

Not confined to the politics of mid-century, however, the core assumptions of the Western were handed down to mid-century filmmakers by the proponents of nostalgic primitivism of the late nineteenth century. They emphasized a primitive lifestyle, anti-capitalism, and masculine virtue in a wild land over the Victorian values of the cities and the bourgeois parlors of the East.

As Western films changed from the silent period to the post-war period, so did they evolve from the classical period to the revisionist period. It is not merely coincidental that as faith in the American nation-state began to break down in the wake of Watergate and the Vietnam War, the classical Western formula grew out of favor. It was replaced by a revamped style of Westerns that saw corruption where the classical Western saw virtue, and despair where the classical Western posited hope. The legacy of the Victorians became more complex in the later Westerns as the genre shifted away from the more established formulas.

Among the Westerns still being made today, the original formula often remains largely intact, however, and although the Little House series proved that a dramatic history of the frontier need not be about showdowns and law and order imposed at the point of a gun, that image continues to shape American ideas about the nation's history and from where order and prosperity have their origins.

Today, the Western has been largely replaced by zombie films, superhero epics, and gritty police dramas. Zombie films provide similar story lines to the Indian extermination narratives of cavalry Westerns, while superheroes act as modern gunfighters on a global stage. Police dramas continue to offer righteous indignation for the viewer in the face of repugnant outlaws. The Western is more powerful than these other genres, however, because it purports to be a type of American history. Although it does not reflect the reality of the historical American frontier, the Western continues to form the imaginations of viewers regarding the role of the American state and American society in the modern world.

Index

Ford, John, ii-iv, 8, 11, 17,
37-39, 43, 59, 66-67, 69-71,
73, 78-81, 87, 92, 94, 96, 98,
104n92, 109-110
Fort Apache, 11, 17, 32, 37-38,
43, 45, 59, 62, 65
Frederick, John T., 51n60
Freeman, Morgan, 103
The Furies, 10

The Grapes of Wrath, iii
Goodnight, Charles, 1, 115
*The Good, The Bad, and the
Ugly*, v, 86, 90, 98
Gottfried, Paul, 12, 12n17
Grassle, Karen, 107
Grey, Zane, 2n2, 51
Griffith, D.W., 57, 58n70

Hackman, Gene, 87
Harris, Richard, 103
Hart, William, S., 58-59
Hartley, L.P., v
Hartwell, R.M., 35n44
Hatfields & McCoys, i
Hathaway, Henry, 74
Hawks, Howard, ii, 10-11,
31, 46, 59, 61, 67, 80, 82, 84,
92, 109
Hawthorne, Nathaniel, 51,
51n60
Hell on Wheels, 4, 4n7
Heston, Charlton, 86
*Hiawatha: The Indian Passion
Play*, 57

High Noon, 61, 66, 73, 79, 83-
84, 85, 94, 116
High Plains Drifter, 89-90, 112
Hill, P.J., 21, 22n25
Hobbes, Thomas, 42, 93-95
Hobsbawm, Eric, 12, 12n16,
48
Hollon, W. Eugene, 21

James, Jesse, 11, 87
Jefferson, Thomas, 13
Jesse James, 34

Kristofferson, Kris, 86

L'amour, Louis, v, 25n31, 26,
63n71
The Lamplighter, 51-52
Landon, Michael, 107
Lane, Rose Wilder, vi, 106,
112-114, 112n98
Leeman, Zachary, 4, 4n7
Leigh, Janet, 61
Lenihan, John, 34, 34n42, 74,
75n78, 84-85
Leone, Sergio, ii, 8, 11, 26,
80, 84, 86, 89-90, 100-102
Little House on the Prairie
(book series), vi, 106
Little House on the Prairie
(television show), 10, 106-
107, 109-115
Locke, John, 15-16, 18, 93-
94, 112

Madison, James, 13, 13n18

ABOUT THE AUTHORS

Ryan W. McMaken is a senior editor at the Mises Institute and has a B.A. in economics and an M.A. in public policy and international relations from the University of Colorado. He was an economist for the state of Colorado for five years and taught political science at Arapahoe Community College in Littleton, Colorado for nine years. He lives in Colorado with his wife and four children.

Paul A. Cantor (1945-2022) was Clifton Waller Barrett Professor of English at the University of Virginia. He was the author of numerous books, including *Shakespeare's Rome: Republic and Empire* (Cornell University Press, 1976); *Gilligan Unbound: Pop Culture in the Age of Globalization* (Rowman and Littlefield, 2001); *Literature and the Economics of Liberty: Spontaneous Order in Culture* (Mises Institute, 2009); *The Invisible Hand in Popular Culture: Liberty vs. Authority in American Film and TV* (University Press of Kentucky, 2012); *Pop Culture and the Dark Side of the American Dream: Con Men, Gangsters, Drug Lords, and Zombies* (University Press of Kentucky, 2019)